Edexcel GCSE

English and English Language

Access

Student Book

Clare Constant
Danuta Reah
Racheal Smith
Consultant: **Geoff Barton**

A PEARSON COMPANY

Contents

Introduction

From Martin Phillips

Welcome to Edexcel English! We've worked hard to plan this course to make English engaging and exciting and to design assessments that really help you to show the skills you have developed.

Whether you're taking GCSE English or English Language, you will have the opportunity to read and write texts about issues that are relevant to the world around you and to study both printed and on-screen texts, such as podcasts, trailers and websites. We expect you to have a personal opinion about all sorts of things you read and to be able to back up your opinion by giving good examples from the text. You have to write interestingly and engagingly in different genres, and we also expect you to be able to both speak and listen in a variety of contexts.

This book has been designed to help you to get the best possible grade in GCSE English or English Language. It's tailored to helping you develop your basic skills and is full of tasks that will help you to get better at doing various parts of English. We have tried to make the activities enjoyable and interesting, and we hope they will encourage you to carry on reading, writing and communicating long after your GCSE English is done and dusted, as well as helping you to get a good grade in your GCSE.

Good luck with your studies and I hope you get the best possible results!

Martin Phillips

Martin Phillips, Senior Examiner for GCSE English

The Edexcel GCSE English and English Language specifications

Although GCSE English and GCSE English Language are separate qualifications, the Unit 1 controlled assessment task is common to both, and there are other common elements, including Speaking and Listening, and both have a practical writing task in the Unit 2 examination. Here is an overview of the specifications for both GCSE English and GCSE English Language:

Unit 1 English Today (English and English Language)	
Controlled Assessment – 4 hours	
What is this unit worth? 20% of the total marks	
Task 1 – Reading response to two on-screen or printed non-fiction texts on the same theme	
Task 2 – One non-fiction writing task on the same theme as the reading texts	

Unit 2 The Writer's Craft (English)	Unit 2 The Writer's Voice (English Language)
Examination – 2 hours	Examination – 1 hour 45 minutes
What is this unit worth? 40% of the total marks	**What is this unit worth?** 40% of the total marks
Section A – One three-part question on a Shakespeare play	**Section A** – One question on the language features of a non-fiction text or Different Cultures novel
Section B – One three-part question on a Different Cultures novel	**Section B** – One practical writing task
Section C – One practical writing task	

Unit 3 Creative English (English)	Unit 3 Spoken Language (English Language)
Controlled Assessment – 4 hours	Controlled Assessment – 4 hours
What is this unit worth? 40% of the total marks	**What is this unit worth?** 40% of the total marks
Task 1 – Speaking and listening tasks	**Task 1** – Speaking and listening tasks
Task 2 – One poetry reading task	**Task 2** – One spoken language study
Task 3 – One creative writing task in response to a stimulus	**Task 3** – One writing for the spoken voice task

Introduction

How is the book structured?

This book is divided into five units. Units 1 and 2 of this book are common to both GCSE English and GCSE English Language.

Specification	Unit	This book covers ...
English and English Language	Unit 1 English Today: Reading	the non-fiction Reading controlled assessment task.
	Unit 1 English Today: Writing	the non-fiction Writing controlled assessment task.
	Unit 2 The Writer's Craft / The Writer's Voice	the writing task in the exam (Section C of English and Section B of English Language).
English only	Unit 3 Creative English	the creative writing controlled assessment task.
English Language only	Unit 3 Spoken Language	the Spoken Language Study and the Writing for the Spoken Voice controlled assessment tasks.

Each unit is broken down into lessons which introduce the skills and provide stepped activities that help you develop the skills you need.

There are some activities that refer to additional digital resources, such as videos and podcasts, which are available on the ActiveTeach CD-ROM that accompanies this student book. These are to help you prepare for the options in the specifications that require you to respond to or produce digital texts.

Assessment Practice

In each unit there are Assessment Practice activities that allow you to tackle an examination-style question or part of a controlled assessment task. These are followed by ResultsPlus Maximise your marks pages which show you sample student answers to the question you have attempted. There are examiner comments on each sample answer. You can read these before or after you grade your own response to the assessment practice in the ResultsPlus: Self assessment activity.

Regular ResultsPlus activities help students understand what they need to do to improve their grades.

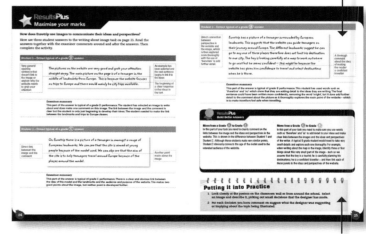

Putting it into Practice activities suggest tasks you could complete to reinforce the skills you have learned.

At the end of each unit is a sample controlled assessment task or examination paper, so that you can see how you will be assessed.

ResultsPlus

These features combine expert advice and guidance from examiners to show you how to achieve better results.

Self assessment – These help you to check your answers to activities to make sure that you have demonstrated the skills you have been practising.

ResultsPlus Self assessment

Check your answer to **Activity 2**. Have you:
- described some small **details** that appear in the image?
- used **'because'**, **'suggests'** or **'implies'** to explain the image?
- linked the image to the **ideas** in the text?
- linked the image to the **audience** and **purpose** of the text?

Exam tip and Controlled assessment tip – These provide advice from examiners to help you know what you can do to improve your results.

ResultsPlus Controlled assessment tip

 Using terms like 'formal' and 'emotive' will help you to persuade your examiner that your answer has shown them a **sound understanding of language**. If you find it too hard to remember the terms, it is still important to say what you think the language is doing in your own words.

Watch out! – These warn you about common mistakes that examiners frequently see students make. Make sure that you don't repeat them!

ResultsPlus Watch out!

Don't just describe what you see! Always use 'because' and explain the effect you've found.

Maximise your marks – These pages show examples of student work that is typical of what might be produced by students whose overall performance was at a grade E, D or C. These examples should help you to understand what you need to do to achieve your target grade.

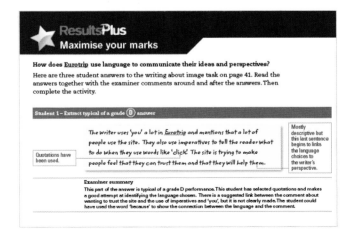

Unit 1 English Today: Reading

Welcome to English Today. This unit is all about English in the world around you – the English you see and use every day of your life.

In this unit, you will develop your skills in reading non-fiction texts. You will read a variety of these texts. Some texts will be printed (like posters, articles or reviews). Some texts will be digital (like podcasts, trailers or websites).

This section of the book will help you to develop your reading skills. You will look at how writers communicate their ideas to their readers.

The texts and activities in this book are designed to help you develop your skills and achieve your target grade in the reading part of your Unit 1 controlled assessment task.

Your assessment

Unit 1 is a controlled assessment unit. You will have **two hours** to complete **one** reading task. You can write up to 1000 words. The task will ask you to write about two different texts, on the same theme, from a choice of six. You will have had the opportunity to study these texts in advance.

Your response to the task must show that you can:

✔ compare two texts

✔ select appropriate details from the texts to support your ideas

✔ explore how writers use presentation and language to communicate their ideas and perspectives.

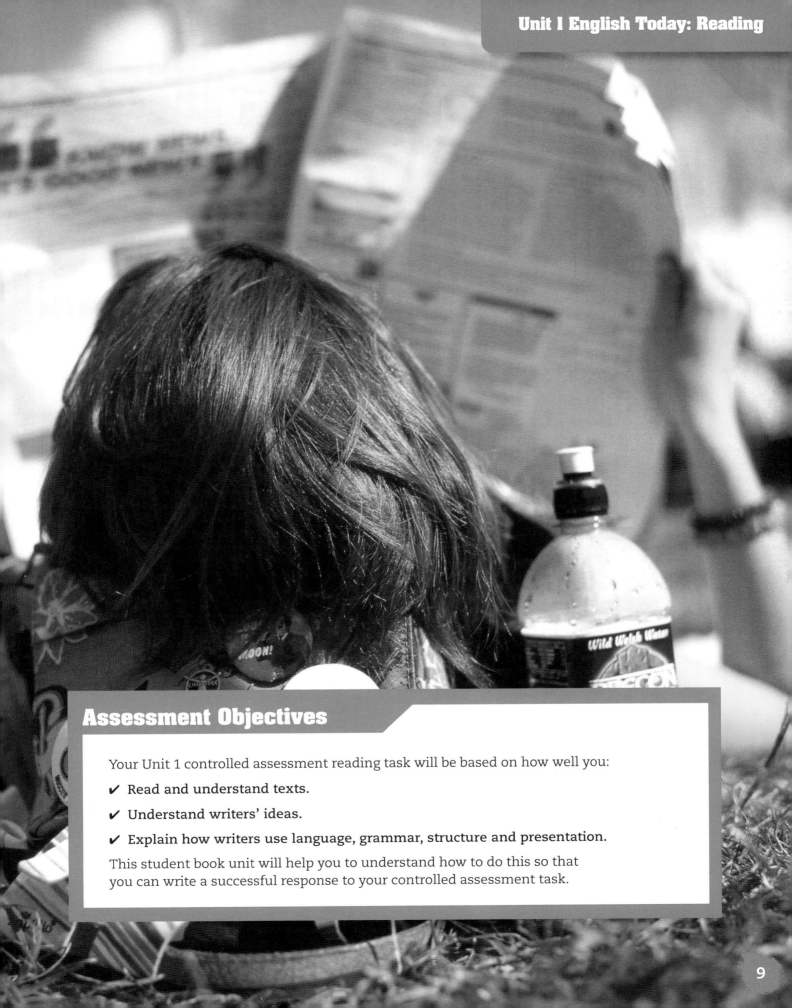

Assessment Objectives

Your Unit 1 controlled assessment reading task will be based on how well you:

✔ Read and understand texts.

✔ Understand writers' ideas.

✔ Explain how writers use language, grammar, structure and presentation.

This student book unit will help you to understand how to do this so that you can write a successful response to your controlled assessment task.

1 Understanding main ideas

This lesson will help you to...

* find the key points in a text

* use the key points in a text to understand what the main ideas are

Before you begin your controlled assessment task you need to understand what the texts are about. To understand a text, you need to first understand its **main ideas**.

Read the article below. Then read the notes underneath it which show how to find the key points in the text.

Are you wrecking your brain?

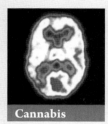
Cannabis

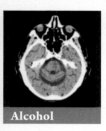
Alcohol

Key point → What exactly are you doing to your brain when you drink alcohol or coffee? If you think they can't be doing much

harm, these pictures may come as a shock. They show that the effects of long term and heavy use can be just as striking as the damage caused by illegal drugs such as cannabis or cocaine. ← Key point They can even result in a pattern of holes in the brain similar to those caused by Alzheimer's disease. The images come from a ← Supporting information remarkable new book – *Change Your Brain – Change Your Life*.

First look closely at any **pictures** that go with the text.

* What is shown in each photograph?

  The first is a brain scan of someone who has taken a lot of cannabis.
  The second shows the brain of someone who has had a lot of alcohol.

* What do the pictures tell you?

  That cannabis and alcohol change your brain.

* How do they tell you this?

  The areas of the brain that are damaged by cannabis and alcohol are highlighted.

Then read the **text**.

* What is the text about?

  It is about how you could be damaging your brain.

* How do you know this?

  The writer says we may be shocked by the harm alcohol and caffeine do to us.

* Decide what the key points of the text are.

  Alcohol and caffeine are more dangerous than you think.
  They can be as bad for your brain as cannabis and cocaine.

ACTIVITY 1

Read the rest of the 'Are you wrecking your brain?' article below.

1 Copy and complete these sentences:

a) *This part of the article is about ...*

b) *I know this because ...*

c) *The key points of this part of the article are ...*

2 Add the key points from both parts of the article together and work out what the main idea of the whole article is. Copy and complete this sentence:

The main idea of the article is ...

Already a bestseller in the US it was written by a neuroscientist and psychiatrist Daniel G Amen, who is a professor of psychiatry and human behaviour at the University of California, Irvine, and the director of the Amen Clinics.

He also runs a programme in Californian schools to make children aware of what recreational drugs can do to their brains. 'They don't believe there could be a problem until they see the pictures and then their response is: 'Omigod!'. That can be enough for them to stop.'

Indeed you might argue that those who want drug classifications loosened should also look closely at these scans.

Some texts in your controlled assessment may be **videos** or **podcasts**. Find the main ideas in these kind of texts by:

- looking at the images
- listening to the words
- listening to the soundtrack.

ACTIVITY 2

A Talk to FRANK video about the effects of cannabis can be found on the ActiveTeach. Watch this video twice.

1 What is the video about?

2 How do you know?

3 List **three** key points.

4 Which student below has understood the video's main idea best – Tom or Deepak?

Tom   **Deepak**

Smoking cannabis seems like fun at first, but it has lots of terrible side effects you won't want.

Cannabis is fun for a while but gets bad.

2 Understanding the writer's perspective

This lesson will help you to...

* work out what the writer's perspective is

You need to be able to explain what a writer's perspective is for your controlled assessment reading task. **Perspective** means what the writer thinks and feels about the subject they are writing about.

Look at this bullying poster and work out the writer's perspective.

First look at the image and work out what it's telling you.

This man is like a jigsaw with missing pieces.

Next read the text and find the writer's main ideas.

The words say bullying takes people apart and it's hard for them to be put back together. So we know that bullying has left the man feeling broken.

Then work out the writer's perspective. Find any words which show the writer's thoughts, beliefs and feelings.

This picture shows that bullying hurts people and 'it's hard' for them to get over it — the writer is showing sympathy for people being bullied and saying bullying is wrong.

WHY DO PEOPLE BULLY?

TO PRETEND THEY ARE TOUGH

TO TRY TO GET OTHERS TO LIKE THEM

TO HIDE THEIR OWN FEARS

THEY COPY OTHERS WHO BULLY

THEY ARE UNHAPPY

THEY DON'T LIKE WHO THEY ARE

ARE THERE ANY OTHER REASONS?

Values Education

ACTIVITY 1

Look at the 'Why do people bully?' poster.

1 What does the writer want readers to think about bullies?

2 Now you have worked out the writer's perspective on bullying. Write it as a sentence that starts like this:

The writer's perspective on bullying is that ...

3 What differences can you find between the perspectives of the writers of the two posters on this page about bullying?

Here is a text that shows a writer's perspective on a film. It is written in the form of an online review.

★HOME   ★FILMS   ★REVIEWS   ★RENTAL

QUANTUM OF SOLACE

Peter Bradshaw, The Guardian ★ ★ ★

I have to confess that this second Bond adventure disappointed me a little: it's not nearly as smart as Craig's debut. There is not much storyline or romance.

What *Quantum of Solace* does have is Daniel Craig. No one could deny Craig's charisma and the effortless way he has inhabited the role. He has some spectacular action sequences and a fair few close-quarter punch-ups in the manner of Bourne, along with some athletic rooftop-leaping chase scenes that Bonds of an earlier vintage would have rejected as being too much like hard work.

Quantum of Solace isn't bad, but from now on, Craig's Bond has to be a real character with something real at stake, however absurd.

ACTIVITY 2

Read the *Quantum of Solace* online review above.

1 Pick out **two** main ideas.

2 What do you think the writer's perspective is? Pick out **three** words from the review that tell you this.

3 Below are two explanations of the writer's perspective. Which explanation do you agree with most? Why?

Explanation 1

The writer thinks <u>Quantum of Solace</u> is disappointing because there is no romance and it does not have a strong storyline, but he likes Daniel Craig.

Explanation 2

This writer thinks <u>Quantum of Solace</u> is too much like other action hero films and what you want in a Bond film is missing.

ACTIVITY 3

1 Find **four** different texts that you can study. These texts can be a poster, magazine article, website, letter or another type of text.

2 Work out each writer's perspective. Complete a table like the one shown here.

	Letter	Text 2	Text 3	Text 4
The writer's perspective	It's important for all students to arrive on time and in the correct uniform.			
How do I know the writer's perspective	The opening sentence of the first paragraph says ...			

3 Audience and purpose

This lesson will help you to...

* work out who a text is written for – the audience

* recognise what the writer's aim is – the purpose

The **audience** of a text is who it's aimed at and written for. Writers will have an audience in mind as they write.

In your controlled assessment you need to be able to work out:

* **who** the target audience of the text is.

* **how** the audience is expected to respond to the text.

Look at the *Freshwater Fishing* magazine cover.

First look at the image and work out **who** it is aimed at.

It is aimed at men who like fishing.

Then look at the image and text to find:

* any other **information about the readers**

  They are in Australia.

* what **sort of vocabulary** the writer is using

  quite informal, uses slang and fishing terms – 'grubbin' and 'wormin'

* what the writer thinks the audience **believes** or is **interested in**.

  catching big fish, different kinds of fish

ACTIVITY 1

Read Text A below and Texts B and C on page 15. Answer the following questions for each text.

1 Who is the audience?

2 What features of the text make it suitable for this audience – for example, language, images, content, etc.?

Text A

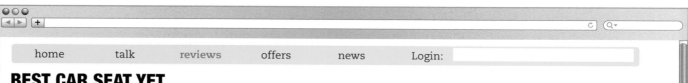

| home | talk | reviews | offers | news | Login: |

BEST CAR SEAT YET

This is my third car seat and by far the best. I have big babies and my first son had to go in the car seat for babies over 9 months as soon as he could sit because he was too big, which annoyed me as it's much safer for him to be rear-facing. For my second son we had the Jane Rebel car seat but by 5 months his shoulders were squashed. Then we got this seat which is just fantastic. With the adjustable headrest it gives better head protection and my son is now nearly 10 months and still rear-facing, even though he's large for his age. The Isofix fixings take away all the hassle and worry from fitting. It's a breeze and can easily be done in 10 minutes. Expensive, but you will get more use from it than many others.

Text B

Text C

Listen to the road safety podcast on the ActiveTeach:

I don't have a first memory, because after the accident, I lost all my childhood memories basically, so all of that's been wiped out as a result of the accident that I had when I was 11 …

Texts are written for a **purpose**. There are many words used to help us describe a text's purpose. Some are listed in the box below.

persuade	explain	argue
advise	review	comment
inform	analyse	entertain

- Some texts try to **get a response** from their audience. For example, they persuade the audience to agree with the writer's perspective.

- Other texts try to **do something** for the audience. For example, they inform the audience about how to use the camera on a mobile phone.

- Some texts have **more than one purpose**. For example, an advertisement persuades the audience to buy the product and may entertain them as well.

ACTIVITY 2

Look at the nine purposes listed in the box above.

1 Sort the purposes into these two groups:

Texts with these purposes want to get a response from their audience	Texts with these purposes want to do something for their audience
persuade	inform

4 Purpose

You will need to work out what a text's **purpose** is in your controlled assessment. Study the Toyota Prius review and identify its purpose.

NEWSONLINE

| news | comment | business | entertainment | **reviews** |

Toyota Prius: The earth's new best friend
Ray Hutton

The Prius is a larger five-door hatchback with a smart modern style and exceptionally good aerodynamics that will do 100mph and also has lower emissions and improved fuel economy — 65.7mpg on the combined cycle (over a mix of town and country driving). The new Prius is top, or rather bottom, of the carbon dioxide emitting league, with an overall figure of 104gm/km, which is better than the most efficient small diesels.

© The Times 07.12.2003/nisyndication.com

First study the text carefully. Search for its key points to work out the writer's perspective.

It's a review telling readers about the Prius's engine, style and benefits. The writer thinks the car is good.

Next decide why the writer has written it.

The writer wants readers to make an informed decision about buying the car.

Then use what you have found out to identify the text's purpose.

The text's purpose is to inform and review.

ACTIVITY 1

Read the five texts on page 17.

1 Decide which of the following purposes best describes each text.

| inform | entertain | comment | persuade | review |

2 Write a sentence explaining in detail each text's purpose. Use examples from the text to support your answer. The first one has been done for you.

Text A: The purpose of the text is to inform people so that when they cook on a barbecue they can make sure the food is properly cooked. It's also meant to be entertaining so readers will want to keep reading to the end to find all the information.

Text A

The Food Standard Agency's website, available on the ActiveTeach.

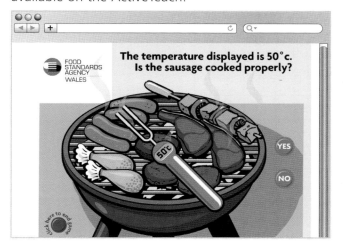

Text B

The Be Humankind video, available on the ActiveTeach.

Text C

HOME   HOW TO   VIDEO

How to be the life of the party

Step 1 Dress to kill. Wear something either very fashionable or very flashy (but tasteful). Well-tailored clothes imply class; bold outfits are hard to forget.

Step 2 Make a grand entrance – carry a kazoo and announce your arrival with a fanfare. Better yet, provide your friends with kazoos and let them do it for you.

Step 3 Stand up straight and look people directly in the eye. Self-assurance is very attractive. If you have to fake it, then fake it. It gets easier the more you practise. People will believe that there must be some underlying reason for your self-confidence.

Text D

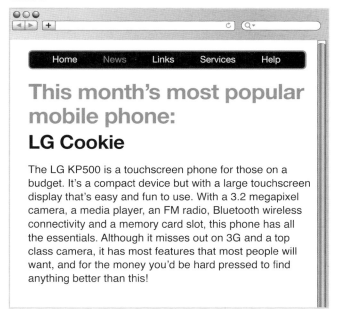

Home   News   Links   Services   Help

This month's most popular mobile phone:

LG Cookie

The LG KP500 is a touchscreen phone for those on a budget. It's a compact device but with a large touchscreen display that's easy and fun to use. With a 3.2 megapixel camera, a media player, an FM radio, Bluetooth wireless connectivity and a memory card slot, this phone has all the essentials. Although it misses out on 3G and a top class camera, it has most features that most people will want, and for the money you'd be hard pressed to find anything better than this!

Text E

Should Rafa be sacked?

How dare you ask such things. Mr Benitez (as he should be addressed) is one of the most successful Liverpool managers and should be respected for his achievements and management skills. He is not a man that bows to media or fan pressure.

Liverpool Football Club is a club with strong tradition and a loyal fan base, and the true Liverpool Fans should get behind the Manager and not undermine him. Remember he is the man who convinced 'El Nino' (Torres) to wear the Red of Liverpool, and he was the man who convinced Gerrard to snub the money bags of the Chelski.

Although Liverpool are facing a financial crisis, it is important that Liverpool supporters remember there is no other club like ours. So even if you disagree with Mr Benitez's tactics, his insistence to play two holding midfielders or one lone striker (although he is good enough to do so), we should get behind him and the team and remember that 'You will never walk alone'.

A **True** Liverpool fan

5 Understanding presentation

This lesson will help you to...

* recognise different presentational features

* understand the effect of presentational features

Writers present their texts in ways that will help them get their ideas across. You need to notice which **presentational features** the writer used and then work out the effect of these.

Here are some examples of presentational features:

headings	text boxes	font size	font colour
bullet points	borders	images	numbering
font	shapes	background	captions

ACTIVITY 1

Look at the two posters (Text A and Text B). Both posters are advertising music festivals.

1 What do you notice first about each poster?

2 Which of the presentational features in the box above are used in Text A?

colour, background ...

3 Which of the presentational features in the box above are used in Text B?

Text A

Text B

You need to understand **how** presentational features are used. This means noticing details about each feature, such as the style of the font or the position in the text.

ACTIVITY 2

Look again at the musical festival posters.

1 Look at the presentational features you selected in Activity 1 questions 2 and 3. List the details of how these features are used in each text.

Text A: colour — dark brown, background — plain

2 Note down all your ideas about what these details suggest to the reader. For example:

The dark brown font on the Hop Farm Festival poster is like brown earth or trunks of trees so it gives it a natural feel.

ACTIVITY 3

Look again at Text A and Text B. Each poster uses presentational features in a particular way to tell readers what the advertised festival will be like.

1 Find **five** differences in the way presentational features are used in the two posters.

2 What idea or impression does this give about the festival? Copy and complete the chart below.

How presentational features are used	What impression this gives in Text A	What impression this gives in Text B
1 *Use of colour*	*Pale brown background feels natural so you think the music will be …*	*Primary colours — like a rainbow. Makes you think the festival will be varied with different sorts of music*
2		
3		
4		
5		

3 Write a sentence stating the effect of the way each feature is used. You could start like this:

The brightly coloured boxes and fonts in Text B suggest that the music will be lively and there will be …

4 What overall impression of the festival do the presentational features in Text A give?

5 What overall impression of the festival do the presentational features in Text B give?

6 Exploring the effects of presentation

This lesson will help you to...

* understand the effect of different presentational features

* work out how presentational features support the text's main ideas

You need to work out how the presentation of a text helps to communicate the writer's ideas and perspective. Look at the poster below.

First read the text. Work out what the main ideas are and what the writer's perspective is.

You can get 25% off Odeon cinema tickets. Readers will enjoy watching films at Odeon cinemas.

Next notice how presentational features are used. Work out what they suggest.

Using the colour blue for the photograph links to the colour of the Odeon logo because it's like the blue light that shines from the projector when you are in the cinema.

Then decide how these suggestions help to communicate the main ideas and the writer's perspective.

Using blue links the feeling of enjoying the cinema experience with the Odeon brand and with the offer, which stands out in white writing against the blue background. All this helps to get across the main offer and the writer's perspective, which is that readers will really enjoy Odeon cinemas.

 ResultsPlus **Watch out!**

■ Don't just describe what you see! Always use 'because' and explain the effect you've found.

ACTIVITY 1

Study the NSPCC home page below.

1 Decide what the writer's main ideas and perspective are. Copy and complete these sentences:

The main ideas are that the NSPCC works to …

The writer's perspective is that the readers should …

2 Make a chart like the one below. List **five** of the presentational features used in the home page. Make a note of what you think they suggest.

Presentational feature	What it suggests
1 Coloured background and font — bright green for the top and white writing …	It's bright and positive — green for go like a traffic light or green like nature. White suggests …
2 Images —	

3 Write sentences that show how each of the presentational features used support the text's main ideas and perspective. You may want to begin like this:

The NSPCC wants it to feel natural to stop child cruelty. Using … helps because it suggests …

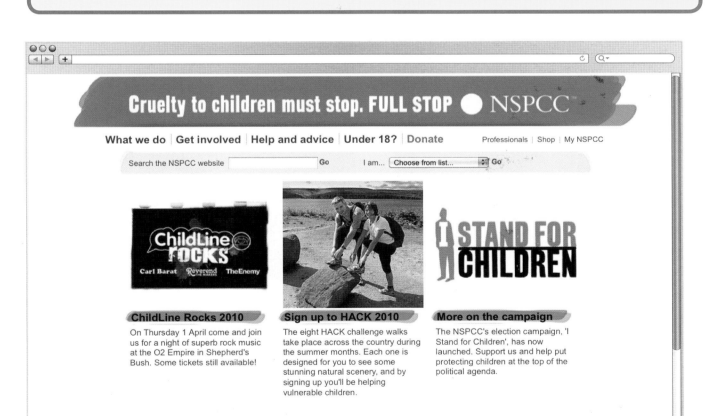

7 Commenting effectively on presentation

This lesson will help you to...

* compare the way presentational features are used in texts

* comment on presentation effectively

You need to be able to compare the way presentational features are used in different texts. Follow these steps:

First note down for each text the main ideas and the writers' perspectives.

Next make a chart showing how for each text the presentational features help to communicate the writers' ideas and perspectives.

Then use your notes to write sentences comparing how the different presentational features help each writer communicate their ideas and perspectives.

Text A

Did you know?

* **On average 1,400 fires per year occur in caravans.**
* **More than five fires a day are started by candles.**
* **Every three days someone dies from a fire caused by a cigarette.**

These tips will help keep you and your family safe from fire.

Text B

Frances the Firefly says never play with matches!

FIRE KILLS YOU CAN PREVENT IT

ACTIVITY 1

Study the two posters on page 22.

1 What are the main ideas and perspectives of each poster? What audience is each poster aimed at?

2 Copy and complete the chart below. Add notes on how colour is used in Text B. Then add notes on how images and fonts are used in the two posters.

3 Next add notes to your chart explaining how each presentational feature helps the writer to communicate their ideas and perspective.

4 In the last column of your chart, write a sentence comparing how each presentational feature is used in Texts A and B.

Feature	Text A	Text B	Comparison
Coloured background, images and font	<u>How is it used?</u> Big colour photograph with burnt black caravan and eye-catching bright orange flames. <u>How does it help communicate the ideas and perspective?</u> Bright orange makes the fire feel like a real danger.	<u>How is it used?</u> Uses soft blue colours for the background … <u>How does it help communicate the ideas and perspective?</u> Background colour makes the poster appealing to …	Both posters use bright orange to get across the idea that fire is a real danger. Text B also uses softer colours which make it look like a story book and will appeal to children.
Images			
Font			

ResultsPlus Controlled assessment tip

Try starting your paragraphs by using words from the task you have been given. For instance:

> • Comment on how the writers use presentation and language

The writer of this text has used presentational features to …

Connectives are words that join phrases together. They are useful for comparing texts, by saying what is different or similar.

Use these connectives to help you explain what is **different**:

but	however	on the one hand ... on the other hand

For example:

In Text A the writer uses lots of text in a bulleted list to provide information. However, in Text B the writer uses just a few words to give children a clear message.

Use these connectives to help you explain what is **similar**:

and	also	similarly	in the same way

For example:

In Text A the writer uses a photograph to grab the readers' attention. Similarly, in Text B the writer uses a cartoon character to appeal to children.

ACTIVITY 2

Study Texts A and B on page 22 again. Copy and complete the sentences below.

1 Use the connective '**however**' in a sentence to explain the different main ideas and perspectives in Texts A and B.

The main ideas and perspective in Text A are ... However, in Text B ...

2 Write three sentences comparing the different effects of the images used each text. You could start like this:

The image in Text A is of a ... while the image in Text B shows ...

In Text A there is a real fire but in Text B ... which has the effect ...

3 Write three sentences comparing the effects that the fonts have in each text. You could start like this:

In Text B the writer uses a large font to ... This suggests ...

4 Explain in a sentence how each writer's use of colour, images and fonts supports their ideas and perspective. Begin your sentences like this:

In Text A, using the image of ... supports the writer's idea that ...

In Text B, using the image of a ... supports the writer's idea that ...

Assessment Practice

As part of your controlled assessment task you should explore how the writers communicate their ideas and perspectives using presentation.

ACTIVITY 3

Look at the Eurotrip webpage and write a response to this question.

1 How does the Eurotrip webpage use presentation to communicate their ideas and perspectives?

You should spend 10 minutes on this task.

 ResultsPlus Self assessment

Before you complete this self-assessment activity you might like to read some sample answers to this task on the following pages (26 – 27).

Check your answer to Activity 3:
- Did you **select appropriate examples** of presentation or pick out small parts of the text?
- Did you **name the presentational devices** used?

Did you use words such as **'because'** and **'suggests'** to comment on how the presentation used communicates the writer's ideas and perspectives?

Maximise your marks

How does the Eurotrip webpage use presentation to communicate their ideas and perspectives?

Here are three student answers to the writing about presentation task on page 25. The labels around each answer and the summary after are examiner comments. Read both the student answers and examiner comments. Then complete the activity at the bottom of page 27.

> There are some examples picked out but this is only description

There is a logo with an arrow and it is on a blue background. There are loads of words — too many words — it is hard to read - I can't ever be bothered to read this much stuff . There is orange writing. Eurotrip are a company who do holidays. There are loads of pictures of different places. They are all muddled together.

> The comment is irrelevant – having too much writing for the student to read does not link to the ideas or the audience of the website

Examiner summary

This part of the answer is typical of grade E performance. The student has picked out examples of presentation but there is no comment on what Eurotrip were trying to achieve. Some of the comments are irrelevant, and the idea about this being a holiday site is not connected to the pictures of places.

Student 2 – Extract typical of a grade (D) answer

> Describes presentation by picking out examples

In the website Eurotrip have very clear writing and its use is quite smart. For example on the page titled 'the packing list' they have the subheading 'the packing list' in big blue writing and this makes it stand out so you know what this page is going to be about. They have used a lot of space in between paragraphs and have used colour to make the website seem friendly and slightly informal.

> Good comment on writer's perspective but not connected to a particular example

> Some understanding of the ideas connected to a clear example

Examiner summary

This part of the answer is typical of grade D performance. The student has selected examples from the text to demonstrate the ideas the writer is putting forward, which is shown when they comment on the colour of the packing list heading. They only do this once, and the other comments lack a clear link with a particular part of the website, so the student only shows some understanding of this. If the student had commented more about friendliness and pointed to a specific part of the site they would have received a better mark.

A clear understanding of what the writer was trying to achieve, with good links to a particular example

The 'Eurotrip' logo gives off a friendly welcome when you enter the site. The way 'trip' is emphasised is like a plane about to fly off into the sky, linking to the idea of travel. The writer uses this because he is trying to use the logo as a sign to say 'go now!' The effect on the readers would be to help them know what it is about and how it will change their opinion on travelling.

Begins to consider the perspective that the writer was attempting to communicate

Examiner summary

This part of the answer is typical of grade C performance. The student has shown clear understanding of the writer's ideas and has linked this to the example of the logo. The student shows they understand that the writer of the site is communicating on the subject of travelling abroad. They follow this up by explaining the writer's perspective and using the phrase 'go now' to show a sense of excitement the writer wanted to express. The comment changing the reader's opinion of travel also shows an understanding of the writer's perspective, but it is not expressed well enough to be given much credit.

ResultsP**lus**
Build better answers

Move from a Grade Ⓔ to Grade Ⓓ

You need to pick out examples of presentation that help you to talk about the ideas in the website and try to link the examples you choose to a comment about what the writer was trying to do. This is shown in the difference between Student 1 and Student 2. Student 1's answer contains lots of unrelated ideas with no real links. Student 2 made some attempt to connect the examples to the comments they were making about the site.

Move from a Grade Ⓓ to Grade Ⓒ

You need to select a number of specific examples of presentation used by the writer and make sure you comment on how this presentation has been used. This is shown in the difference between Student 2 and Student 3. Student 2's comment tended to be a description of the presentational devices or ideas in the text but they were not connected. Student 3 connected the examples and the ideas much better.

PUTTING IT INTO PRACTICE

1 Explain to a partner, in as few words as possible, what a good response to presentation must include. Try to identify some key areas which you will need to develop.

2 Your home may contain different texts, such as newspapers and leaflets, which use presentation to help communicate their message. Write a paragraph commenting on the use of presentation in a text you have found to practise what you have learned. Then mark your response.

8 Understanding why images are used

This lesson will help you to...

* understand why images are used in texts

* explore the content of images

An **image** in a text is used for a reason. It may be used to appeal to a particular audience but it can also tell a story, explain something, surprise or entertain readers. An image may be used to:

- **show the writer's perspective** – for example, a photo of people at the beach with umbrellas to show how bad the weather is in England in the summer.

- **make the right audience want to read the text** – for example, an illustration in a story book because young children enjoy colour drawings.

- **help the text achieve its purpose** – for example, a map in a leaflet to show where a town is.

Ask yourself these two questions when you want to work out what an image is doing in a text. Answer them in as much detail as you can. Look at this page from a children's story book.

- What does the image show?

  It's a colourful drawing. The pirate's hat is blowing away. His hair is blowing. The parrot is holding on to the wheel.

- What does the image make readers notice and think?

  You notice that the pirate looks upset that he lost his hat. It makes you think he'll try to get it back.

The wind blew and blew and blew. It blew the big hat into the sea.

ACTIVITY 1

Study the image from a science book.

1 What does it show you?

The image shows ...

2 What does it make you notice and think?

The image makes me notice that ...

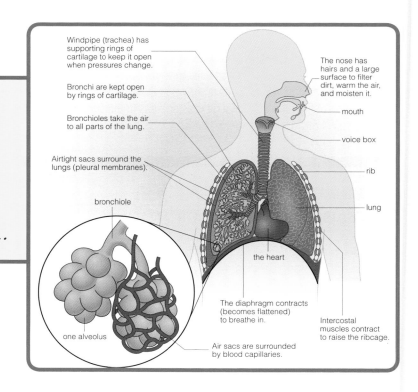

Windpipe (trachea) has supporting rings of cartilage to keep it open when pressures change.

Bronchi are kept open by rings of cartilage.

Bronchioles take the air to all parts of the lung.

Airtight sacs surround the lungs (pleural membranes).

bronchiole

The nose has hairs and a large surface to filter dirt, warm the air, and moisten it.

mouth

voice box

rib

lung

the heart

one alveolus

The diaphragm contracts (becomes flattened) to breathe in.

Air sacs are surrounded by blood capillaries.

Intercostal muscles contract to raise the ribcage.

You need to work out **why** an image is being used in a text.

First read the text and work out its main ideas.

Next work out the writer's perspective and purpose.

Then study the image and work out what it is showing you.

Lastly decide how the image supports what the writer is trying to do.

ACTIVITY 2

Read the leaflet then answer these questions. Copy and complete the sentences to help you.

1 Find **two** key points of the text.

2 Use the key points to decide the text's purpose.

3 Use the key points to decide the writer's perspective.

4 Write a sentence explaining why the text has been written.

The text is written to …

5 What does the image show you?

The image shows …

6 What does the image make readers think or feel?

Readers feel …

7 Explain **three** ways the image supports the purpose of the leaflet.

The image shows readers … which links to the writer's perspective that …

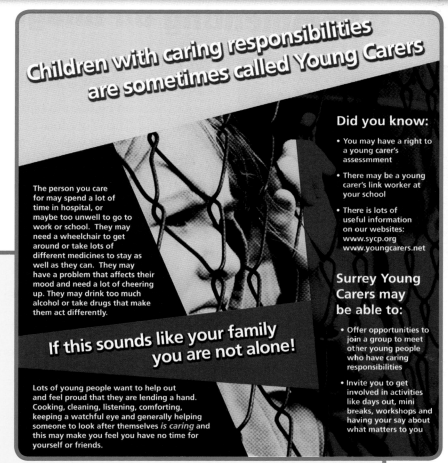

Children with caring responsibilities are sometimes called Young Carers

The person you care for may spend a lot of time in hospital, or maybe too unwell to go to work or school. They may need a wheelchair to get around or take lots of different medicines to stay as well as they can. They may have a problem that affects their mood and need a lot of cheering up. They may drink too much alcohol or take drugs that make them act differently.

If this sounds like your family you are not alone!

Lots of young people want to help out and feel proud that they are lending a hand. Cooking, cleaning, listening, comforting, keeping a watchful eye and generally helping someone to look after themselves *is caring* and this may make you feel you have no time for yourself or friends.

Did you know:

• You may have a right to a young carer's assessment

• There may be a young carer's link worker at your school

• There is lots of useful information on our websites: www.sycp.org www.youngcarers.net

Surrey Young Carers may be able to:

• Offer opportunities to join a group to meet other young people who have caring responsibilities

• Invite you to get involved in activities like days out, mini breaks, workshops and having your say about what matters to you

ResultsPlus Self assessment

Check your answer to **Activity 2**. Have you:
• described some small **details** that appear in the image?
• used **'because', 'suggests' or 'implies'** to explain the image?
• linked the image to the **ideas** in the text?
• linked the image to the **audience and purpose** of the text?

9 Commenting on images

This lesson will help you to...

* explore the way an image is presented

* comment on the effect of an image

The way an image is presented can help you to understand the writer's ideas.

Colour can be used to hint at something without the writer having to say anything. This is because people already have ideas about colours from everyday life. For example, the colour white makes you think of purity, like a wedding dress.

You can explain how images are used by saying what they **suggest**, **imply** or **give an impression** of. Try to use these words when you talk about an image. For example:

* The image gives the impression that ...
* The writer uses green to imply ...
* Using the colour red suggests ...

ACTIVITY 1

Look at the traffic light. Copy and complete these sentences.

1 What do the red and green lights tell drivers?

Red tells drivers to ...

Green tells drivers to ...

2 List any other ideas red and green suggest.

Red also suggests ...

Green also suggests ...

ACTIVITY 2

Study the knife crime poster.

1 What are the main ideas?

2 What is the writer's perspective?

3 Where has the writer used the colour red?

4 What does the use of red suggest to readers?

5 The rest of the poster is in black and white. What might this suggest?

The position or **angle** of an image can suggest ideas too. For example, if you look down at something you may feel more important, but if you are at eye level then you might feel equal.

Where different objects are placed in the image can also hint at ideas. This is called the **composition** of the picture.

- Objects at the **front** are normally the most important.
- Things at the **back** might be less important or may be hidden from notice.

Image A

Image B

ACTIVITY 3

Study Image A and Image B.

1 Which angles are used in Image A and which are used in Image B?

- Looking down on the snake
- Looking up at the snake
- At eye level with the snake

2 What composition is being used? Where is the snake placed in relation to the other objects or people in the picture?

3 What effect does each photograph have? Use your answers about the angle and composition to write your answer.

10 Understanding moving images

When you comment on **moving images**, such as trailers or advertisements, you need to work out what effect the **soundtrack** and **camera shots** have, as well as the images and words used.

A writer chooses which images and sounds to use so that the whole film expresses the writer's ideas and perspective.

Watch the War on Want video about people who make clothing. The video is available on the ActiveTeach.

First watch the whole moving image text. Decide what the writer's main ideas and perspective are.

Then watch each scene. Ask yourself:

* **What is this scene showing me?**

  It's focusing on a clothes factory worker called Parveen who lives in Bangladesh. You see a real person who suffers because of the very low wages she is paid to make clothes that people in the UK buy.

* **What does the soundtrack add to this scene?**

  You can hear Parveen speaking in Bangla. The English voiceover explains what her problem is. She works 80 hours a week for only £6.50.

ACTIVITY 1

Watch the video from the Prince's Trust website on the ActiveTeach.

1 Decide in what order the images on page 33 appear in the video.

2 Watch the video without any sound. Then watch it again with the sound. What difference does the soundtrack make to each image? Record your answers in a chart like the one below.

Image	Soundtrack	Effect
H – Youth leaving his flat	Angry voices	Suggests his home life is unhappy. He is being thrown out. Soundtrack tells you why the youth looks so down.

Image A

Image B

Image C

Image D

Image E

Image F

With guidance, training and motivation
we can help young people find a better path.

Image G

Image H

Image I

Image J

The way a scene is filmed and the type of **camera shots** that are used can produce many different effects. You need to be able to comment on these.

How can you work out what effect the camera shots have?

- A **close up** allows you to connect with the character.

- A **distance shot** makes them seem less important and tells you more about what is going on around them.

For example:

It's shot from above and from a distance. He's at the back with people rushing past him. Filming it like this suggests he's unimportant.

Pick out any other details that strike you. Ask yourself lots of 'Why?' questions about what you see.

Why can't we see his face? Is it to make him seem anonymous? It makes him seem even more lost. Or does he have something to hide? It makes him seem suspicious.

ACTIVITY 2

1. Study **five** of the shots on the previous page. What effect does the way each shot is filmed have on viewers?

2. Watch the Prince's Trust video again. Use what you have learned to write a paragraph about what effect the writer's use of angle, soundtrack and filming has.

   The writer's use of angle gives the impression that ...

3. Which of these sentences best explains the film's perspective? Give reasons for your choice.

   A. It's your fault if you end up in trouble – you made the choices.
   B. Support the Prince's Trust because then a young person's life doesn't have to end up this way.

ResultsPlus Controlled assessment tip

⚠ When commenting on moving images, focus on what **choices** the director has made and why.

Assessment Practice

As part of your controlled assessment task you could explore how the writers use images as presentational devices to communicate their ideas and perspectives.

ACTIVITY 3

Look at the Eurotrip webpage and write a response to this question.

1 How does the Eurotrip webpage use images to communicate their ideas and perspectives?

You should spend 10 minutes on this task.

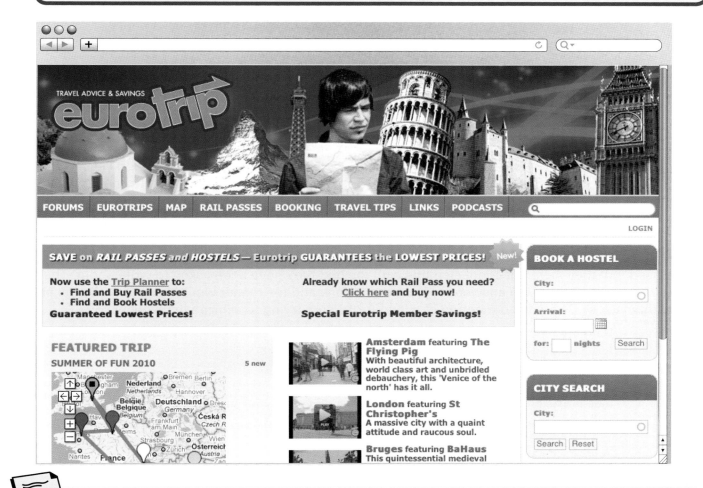

ResultsPlus Self assessment

Before you complete this self-assessment activity you might like to read some sample answers to this task on the following pages (36 – 37).

Check your answer to Activity 3:
- Did you describe the small **details** in the images?
- Did you use **'suggest'** or **'implies'** to explain the choices made by the designer?
- Did you link the images used to the writer's **perspective and ideas**?

Maximise your marks

How does the Eurotrip webpage use images to communicate their ideas and perspectives?

Here are three student answers to the writing about images task on page 35. Around and after the answers are examiner comments. Read both the student answers and examiner comments. Then complete the activity at the bottom of page 37.

Student 1 – Extract typical of a grade E answer

This explains why images are used on a simple level, but the student hasn't linked this to Eurotrip

> Images are pictures and these are part of presentational devices as they are used to present information to the reader. Most designers use them to make things look prettier and easy to look at. I like lots of pictures because they make things easier to read and easier to understand.
>
> The website we have studied uses pictures. There is a man with a map. There are buildings and a map at the bottom.

This is just description. There is no comment on the ideas and perspectives on the Eurotrip site

Examiner summary

This part of the answer is typical of grade E performance. The student has made some comments on how images are used, but they have not connected this with the text they have been asked to write about. The examples in the second part of the answer are just descriptions and the reader would have to make the link to the ideas themselves. There is no mention of what Eurotrip are trying to achieve in the website.

Student 2 – Extract typical of a grade D answer

Very general opening sentence that doesn't link the image or explain why the website needs to grab your attention

> The pictures on the website are very good and grab your attention straight away. The main picture on the page is of a teenager in the middle of landmarks from Europe. This is because the website focuses on trips to Europe and there would mainly be city trips available.

An example has been selected and the next sentence begins to link it to the ideas

The beginning of a clear response to the ideas in the text

Examiner summary

This part of the answer is typical of grade D performance. The student has selected an image to write about and does make one comment on this image. The link between the image and the comment is clear but the student is only just beginning to develop their ideas. The student needed to make the link between the landmarks and trips to Europe more clear.

Direct link between the image and the comment

On *Eurotrip* there is a picture of a teenager in amongst a range of European landmarks. We can see that the site is aimed at young people because of the model used. We can also see that the aim of the site is to help teenagers travel around Europe because of the places around the model.

Another point made about the image

Examiner summary

This part of the answer is typical of grade C performance. There is a clear and obvious link between the idea of the model and the landmarks and the audience and purpose of the website. The student makes two good points about the image, but neither point is developed further.

ResultsPlus
Build better answers

Move from a Grade Ⓔ to Grade Ⓓ
In this part of the task you need to make sure that the comments you make about images link to the text you have been studying and the comments should be linked to the examples that you select. Don't just describe parts of the text without making any comment on them. This is shown in the difference between Student 1 and Student 2. Student 1's answer has lots of unrelated ideas with no real links. Student 2 made some attempt to connect the examples they chose to the comments they were making about the site.

Move from a Grade Ⓓ to Grade Ⓒ
In this part of the task you need to clearly comment on the links between the image and the ideas and perspectives in the website. This is shown in the difference between Student 2 and Student 3. Although these students make very similar points, Student 3 obviously connects the age of the model used to the intended audience of the website.

PUTTING IT INTO PRACTICE

1 Look closely at the posters on the classroom wall or around the school. Select an image and describe it, picking out small decisions that the designer has made.

2 For each decision the designer has made, explain what you think the designer was suggesting or implying about the topic being illustrated.

11 Understanding language choices

This lesson will help you to…

* recognise what language choices the writer made

* recognise how language choices suit the writer's audience, purpose, main ideas and perspective

Glossary of language features

Standard English: the most widely accepted form of the English language

Slang: words or phrases that are used by particular groups of people only

Formal language: language used for an official audience

Informal language: language used for a casual audience

Technical words: words for a certain trade or profession

Emotive language: words that appeal to the emotions

Alliteration: words that begin with the same sound

Direct address: saying the name of the person being spoken to

---

You need to be able to comment on the **vocabulary** and **language features** used in a text. You should work out how they suit the text's audience and purpose and help the writer express the main ideas and perspective.

ACTIVITY 1

Read Texts A, B and C on page 39.

1. What vocabulary and language features are highlighted in each text? Use the terms in the box to help you.

slang	formal	informal	standard English	describing words	verbs
fact	opinion	emotive	alliteration	technical words	direct address

Record your answers in a chart like this:

Text	Type of vocabulary/language feature	Example
A	slang describing words and opinion	quirky cute so delish you'll wanna eat it!
B	technical words	manual or F1 gear changes

2. Use a chart like the one below to list each text's main ideas, perspective, purpose and audience.

Text	Main idea	Perspective	Purpose	Audience
A	There's a free lip gloss with this edition of Mizz.	It's an exciting flavour and smells great so don't miss out.	To persuade people to buy the magazine.	Teenage girls
B				

3. Write two sentences about each text to explain how the vocabulary used suits the text's main ideas, perspective, purpose and audience. The first one has been done for you.

Text A: Text A is for teenage girls and it's meant to persuade them to buy Mizz magazine, which has a free lip gloss on it. Using slang like 'cute' and 'so delish' shows teenagers the magazine will speak their language which helps persuade them to buy it too.

Text A

Go balmy! How quirky cute is this Mizz lip balm? It comes in yummy Strawberry Milkshake flavour and smells so delish you'll wanna eat it! Probably not a good idea though guys, stick to smothering your pout with it instead. Get yours free with this fortnight's mag now!

Text B

The Ferrari Centre in Kent. Probably the best known name for sales and Ferrari servicing in Kent and the destination for all things Ferrari.

The Ferrari Centre has been based on the Parkwood Estate in Maidstone for nearly 20 years and our collection of Ferraris could well be the largest indoor display of used Ferraris under one roof across the whole of the UK.

We specialise in vehicles from the 1970's including the Ferrari 246 Dinos to current models such as the 430s. You can choose from our selection of Spiders, Targa tops, Berlinetta, manual or F1 gear changes and sometimes colour as well, after all - not all Ferraris are red!

| 39

Text C

About Us | Sponsor a Dog | Dog Breeds | **Rehoming** | Donate

REHOMING

The health and happiness of every dog is at the heart of all our efforts and we try to find each and every dog in our care a loving home for life. We never destroy a healthy dog.

Visit our rehoming section to find your nearest Dogs Trust Rehoming Centre.

ResultsPlus Controlled assessment tip

Using terms like 'formal' and 'emotive' will help you to persuade your examiner that your answer has shown a **sound understanding of language**. If you find it too hard to remember the terms, it is still important to say what you think the language is doing in your own words.

12 Commenting on sentences

In your controlled assessment you need to comment on the **types of sentence** writers use to express their ideas and perspectives. To do this, you need to be able to identify the different kinds of sentence:

command	Get a cheap one you won't mind losing.
question	Which phone should you buy?
list	It'll get nicked, borrowed, broken and go out of fashion before you blink.
exclamation	The cheapest to run, of course!
short sentence	The trendy one is no good.

When you have identified a type of sentence, ask yourself:

* How does using this type of sentence here help the writer express their ideas or perspective?

* What effect does it have on the reader?

ACTIVITY 1

Look at the list of sentence types above.

1 What type of sentence would you use to:

a) show the writer feels strongly about something

exclamation

b) tell people to do something

c) give reasons to back up a point

d) grab the reader's attention or to get them to agree with the writer?

ACTIVITY 2

Read the article 'Why I hate Facebook' on page 41.

1 Which of these types of sentence does the writer use? Re-write each type of sentence you find in the article and label it.

command	question	list	exclamation	short sentence

2 Which of these statements best explains how the writer uses different sentence types to express her ideas and perspectives? Why?

a) She uses questions to get the reader thinking about her point of view and uses lists to include lots of proof that her points are sensible.

b) She uses questions because she doesn't know the answer and uses lists so that she can include lots of points.

Janet Street-Porter: Why I hate Facebook

Nothing sums up the shallow world we live in more than a group of people chatting away to each other for hours each day via sites like Bebo, MySpace and Facebook.

Have these sad characters got nothing better to do? What is it about the real world that they find so unappealing?

I am proud to say I have real friends, with their little weird ways, their shortcomings, their obsessions, their strange eating habits and their wonderful gossip.

We have our feuds and our periods of 'non speakers' from time to time (I admit I am not the easiest person in the world to get on with), but I know that if I feel a bit lonely, or need cheering up, I can call one of them up, have a chat, meet for a meal or a drink, and afterwards I'll feel better.

ACTIVITY 3

Watch the 'Giving blood' video on the ActiveTeach.

Leukaemia treatment
starts Thursday week 8am

1 Work out the text's purpose, main ideas and the writer's perspective.

2 What types of sentence did the writer use in the script?

3 Copy and complete these two sentences to explain:

a) why the writer made these choices: *The writer uses ... because ...*

b) the effect of these choices: *This has the effect of ...*

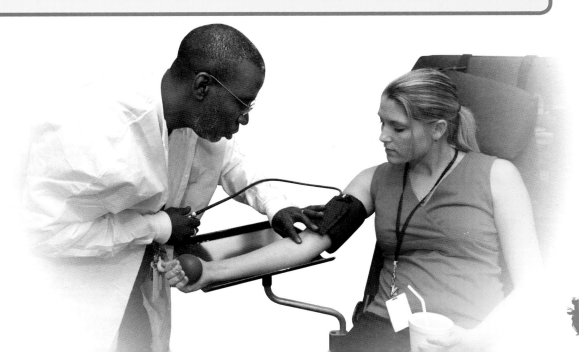

13 Commenting on a writer's language

This lesson will help you to...

* understand how writers use different language features and sentence types

* explain what effect the writer's choices have

In your controlled assessment you need to explain how the writer's choice of **language** helps to communicate their ideas and perspectives.

First identify the different types of sentence and vocabulary used. Has the writer used lists, commands, exclamations, short sentences, or questions? Is the vocabulary formal, informal, technical, descriptive, or humorous?

Then work out exactly how each of the language features you spotted helps the writer to express their ideas and perspective, or to suit the audience and purpose.

When you find describing words ask yourself:

What does this word suggest about the writer's feelings or attitude?

ACTIVITY 1

Read the article 'Trek's new TT bike' on page 43.

1 Who is the audience?

2 What are the main ideas and perspective?

3 What types of sentence does the writer use? What effect do they have?

4 What sort of vocabulary does the writer use? How is it suitable for the audience?

5 Copy and complete the speech bubble below as though you were the writer of the text. Choose words from the box and an example from the article to fill in the blanks.

formal	language	facts	opinions
humour	technical language	informal language	slang

I used . . . . because my readers know what it means. Using . . . .
. . . . lets me refer to things quickly without having to explain them in detail and it makes me seem knowledgeable!

I used the phrase '. . . . .' because I wanted to suggest to readers that they can't get this information anywhere else.

As well as facts, I include a lot of my . . . . because I want to sound like an expert.

TREK'S NEW TT BIKE

This is the new Trek time trial bike that Alberto Contador rode in the Dauphine Liberté TT last week. Needless to say, our snapper Graham Watson wasn't allowed to take static photographs of it, but he did manage to get some exclusive spy shots from the motorbike when Contador was on the course.

The Trek TTX has been around for a good four years now, and with Giant, Scott, Specialized, Cervelo and Felt creating ever more imaginative solutions, it was high time Trek came up with an answer. It's probably no coincidence that the new design is ready for Lance Armstrong's Tour de France comeback.

The new Trek TT bike presents a very low profile. From this angle it is possible to see the brake pads emerging directly from the insides of the fork blades.

© *Cycling Weekly*/IPC+Syndication

These words will help you explain clearly what effect a language feature has:

suggests	hints	implies	because	as
suits	adds	strengthens	helps	shows that
makes you feel	underlines	points out		

For example, the expression 'needless to say' **suggests** the reader understands how spying on the latest version of bikes works.

ACTIVITY 2

Read the 'Trek's new TT bike' article again.

1 Write a sentence explaining why the writer used a list in his second paragraph.

Hint: how does it help him express his idea and perspective?

DANCING IS RUBBISH

Overrated, sweaty, rubbish, rubbish, it's for people who feel attractive and people whose arms and legs don't jerk away from their bodies like mine do, like teenagers ashamed to be seen with their mums. It's not right and it's not OK, especially in public, a place where some of us eat. If one must dance, I'd hope one'd have the decency to do it alone in one's bedroom, where only the dolls and JLS posters are there to see. How dare Arlene attempt to inflict dance on us, we who are clumsy and shame-filled and heavy on our feet. Imagine the humiliation of a village forced to polka. Imagine the smell.

© Guardian News & Media Ltd. 2008

ACTIVITY 3

Read the article 'Dancing is rubbish'.

1 Pick out **five** words or phrases that show the writer's attitude towards dancing.

2 Copy and complete the sentence below to explain the effect of one of the words or phrases you picked out.

The writer uses the word … because this suggests …

3 Write **four** sentences of your own explaining the effect of the other words or phrases you picked out.

4 Find **two** different types of sentence used in the dancing article. Explain why the writer has used each type. Copy and complete the sentence below for each sentence type.

In line … the writer has used a … which has the effect of …

ResultsPlus Self assessment

Check your answer to **Activity 3**. Have you:
- picked out an **appropriate** example from the text?
- identified the language that the writer has used?
- used '**because**' to help you comment on the language used?
- linked your comments to the ideas of the writer?
- linked your comments to the audience and purpose of the text?

Text A

Text B

NOKIA 5310 COMES WITH MUSIC REVIEW

Phone rating ★★★★ excellent

In a nutshell: This is a good music phone from Nokia that can rival Sony Ericsson's Walkman range. We love the ultraslim, lightweight design, the practical keypad and the hot looks. The 5310 has a fully loaded music player and FM radio, up to 4 Gbytes of memory for storing songs, a 2 megapixel camera and Bluetooth connectivity. The battery life is below average, but this phone is definitely worth a look, especially the **Comes With Music** edition that gives you a whole year of unlimited free music downloads. Outstanding value for money.

Best buy: On Pay as you Go from the **Carphone Warehouse (Comes With Music)** at £82.18.

Review: October 2008. Last updated July 2009.

Oh yes! Nokia's XpressMusic range has moved up a gear and Sony Ericsson had better watch out. The Nokia 5310 XpressMusic is a classic-shape music phone available in a choice of red or blue. It's an ultrathin phone, at just 9.9 mm, and has a lovely practical design with a good sized conventional keypad and a 5-way navigation key (Sony Ericsson take note!) There are three dedicated music keys placed at the side of the screen and volume keys along the edge. The bevelled edge makes it easy to hold in your palm, and the red or blue stripes are funky but not over the top. We like the look, we like the feel. This is definitely a phone that you can enjoy even when it's switched off, and it's small and light enough to carry anywhere – jeans pocket, shirt pocket or handbag.

Controlled Assessment Practice

Examiner's tip

This is a sample Unit 1 controlled assessment for GCSE English and GCSE English Language.

Examiner's tip

Your controlled assessment task will be based on a theme. All the questions and texts will focus on that theme.

Examiner's tip

These are the texts provided by Edexcel. You must pick two of these texts.

Turn to page 52 to see two of these texts or to see all six texts visit www.edexcel.com.

Guidance for students: Reading/Studying Written Language (Reading) Task

What do I have to do?

You will complete one reading/studying written language (reading) task on the theme of the environment.

You must complete this task on your own.

How much time do I have?

Following your preparation, you will have up to two hours to complete the task.

How do I prepare for the task?

For the chosen theme:
- select **two** texts from the Edexcel texts provided
- prepare by making notes and planning your response to the task.

Environment texts

1 *Guardian* podcast	2 Aeroplanes and Global Warming article
3 Greenpeace Climate Change webpage*	4 *Your Environment* magazine cover
5 The Great Global Warming Swindle trailer	6 *Times* article on air travel*

What must my response to the task show?

The response must show that you can:
- make comparisons between two environment texts
- select appropriate details from two environment texts to support your ideas
- explore how writers use presentation and language to communicate their ideas and perspectives in two environment texts.

How should I present my response?

A written response of up to 1000 words.

The Reading/Studying Written Language (Reading) Task for the student

Your task is to compare the material from **two** texts on the environment.

In your comparison you must:
- explore how the writers communicate their ideas and perspectives
- comment on how the writers use presentation and language
- include examples to illustrate the points you make.

Examiner's tip

Make sure your response covers these points!

Here are two of the texts provided for this task:

'You don't need to forsake your fun in the sun to help combat climate change.' Jane Knight. *The Times*.

17 November 2007

You don't need to forsake your fun in the sun to help combat climate change

Going green isn't just about the number of flights you make, it's also the type of holiday you choose and how you behave on it.

Jane Knight: *Deputy Travel Editor*

What's to be done? In the week that the UN Secretary General Ban Ki Moon visited Antarctica to be told that an ice sheet covering a fifth of the continent may crumble, we also hear that more travellers are balking at spending extra on holidays to help curb climate change.

And who can blame them? If dinner-table chatter is anything to go by, my friends are sick of hearing that they should forsake their fun in the sun to reduce their carbon footprint. No one wants to feel guilty about taking those well-earned holidays. And why should they, asks a colleague pointedly, when livestock generates more harmful emissions through – er – excessive flatulence than aircraft do?

Already faced with hefty fuel surcharges, passengers are reluctant to shell out more, even if it does help the environment. A study by the travel industry marketing specialist BLM Media showed that 35 per cent of respondents would not pay an extra £20 a holiday to offset carbon emissions, while an even greater 59 per cent would not cut down on the number of times they go abroad. Which is why Qatar Airways' announcement this week that it aims to be the first airline to be powered by a gas-based fuel could be revolutionary. It may not happen – an in-depth study is first needed – but at least this shows that airlines are doing something more than passing the green buck on to passengers. Virgin Atlantic has already announced plans to run a plane on biofuel next year.

Going green, though, isn't just about cutting the number of flights you make or offsetting your carbon emissions. It's also about the type of holiday you choose and how you behave on it. I've lost count of the number of hotels that trumpet their "green" credentials by encouraging you to recycle your bath towels, then change your towels twice daily anyway. I prefer to stay in small lodges or hotels where locals form part of the workforce and where hoteliers become involved in the local community, the kind of place you'll find on the useful website responsibletravel.com.

Eco-tourism doesn't have to be the oxymoron that the wildlife advocate Richard Leakey says it is. But as he points out in this issue, it does need international standards. We know how environmentally friendly washing machines are when we buy them, so why can't tourism be rated in a similar way?

Above all, responsible tourism is about awareness, not necessarily at increased cost. Ten years ago, recycling your rubbish in England was almost unheard of. What we need today is a similar change in attitude towards how we holiday.

The message is starting to trickle through. Just minutes after the New Forest this week took three accolades in the Virgin Holidays Responsible Tourism Awards, organised by Responsibletravel.com, Jamaica's tourism chiefs invited the man behind it all to their country, so they could benefit from his wisdom. Responsible tourism doesn't have to cost more, and it doesn't mean we have to stop travelling, but if we want our children, and our children's children, to benefit from travel as we do, we need to start thinking in a slightly deeper shade of green.

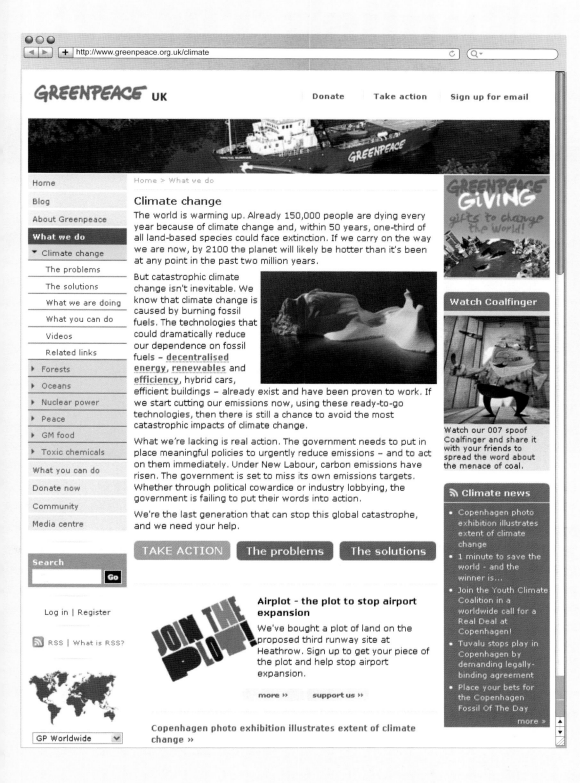

Climate Change webpage
Greenpeace UK

Unit 1 English Today: Writing

This section of the book will help you to develop your writing skills. You will explore how to write for different audiences and purposes. You will also practise expressing your ideas clearly and precisely.

The texts and activities in this unit will help you:

- generate ideas for your writing task
- plan your writing task effectively
- structure your writing
- use engaging vocabulary and sentences.

Developing your writing skills will help you achieve the best grade that you can in your Unit 1 controlled assessment writing task.

Your assessment

This unit is a controlled assessment unit. You will complete **one** writing task. You will have **two hours** to complete the task. You can write up to 1000 words. You will be asked to complete one task from a choice of two. Your writing task will be linked to the theme of your reading task in this unit. You will have had the chance to look at the task and make notes to plan your response in advance so that you feel prepared to complete this part of the controlled assessment.

Your response to the task must show that you can:

✔ make choices in your writing that are appropriate to the audience and purpose

✔ make sure that you spell, punctuate and use grammar accurately and appropriately for the purpose of your writing and to achieve the desired effect.

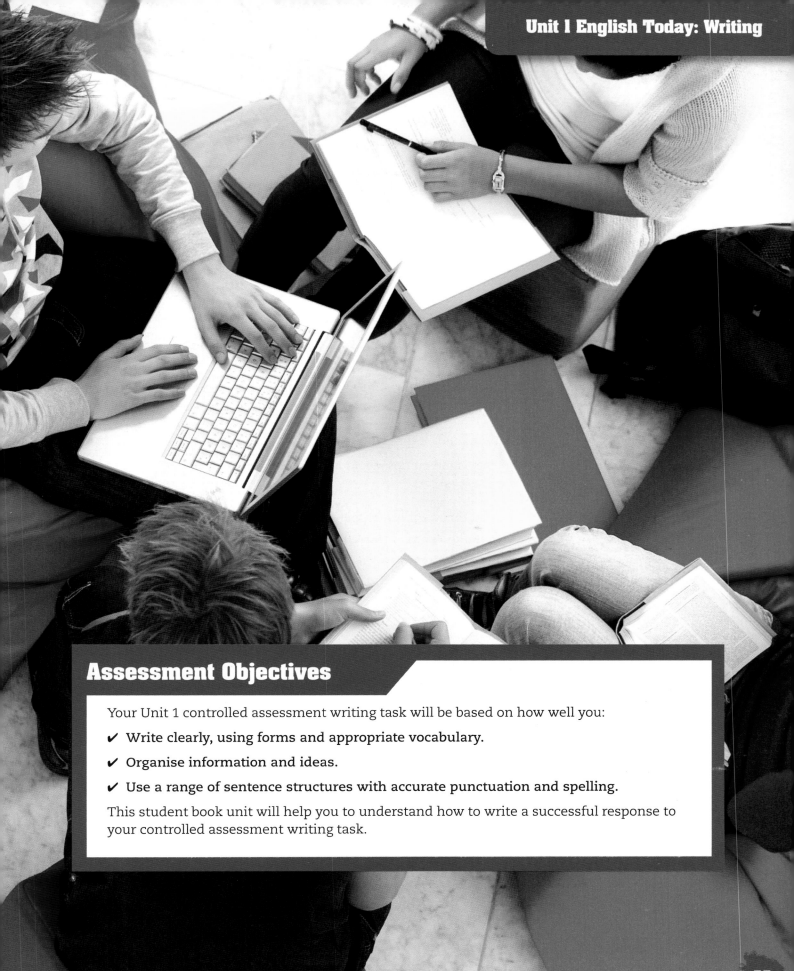

Assessment Objectives

Your Unit 1 controlled assessment writing task will be based on how well you:

✔ Write clearly, using forms and appropriate vocabulary.

✔ Organise information and ideas.

✔ Use a range of sentence structures with accurate punctuation and spelling.

This student book unit will help you to understand how to write a successful response to your controlled assessment writing task.

1 Purpose

This lesson will help you to...

* identify and understand a range of purposes

* know what language features to use in your writing to achieve your purpose

Texts are written for a **purpose**. The purpose is what the writer wants the text to achieve. Writers' purposes include:

* to persuade

* to comment

* to inform

* to argue

* to compare

* to review.

You need to identify the purpose of your controlled assessment writing task and then write in a way that achieves the purpose. Follow these steps:

First read the task.

> Write an article for a magazine in which you persuade readers to take a specific point of view about an environmental issue.

Then ask yourself these questions:

* What is the purpose word in the task?

  persuade

* What do I want my writing to achieve?

  To make readers share my view about an environmental issue, like recycling.

* What do I have to communicate to the audience to achieve this purpose?

  Tell them why they need to recycle – because it will reduce landfill waste.

ACTIVITY 1

Look at the following task.

> Write a podcast for a teenage website informing readers of the dangers of smoking.

1 Work out the task's purpose and how to achieve it.

 a) What is the purpose word in the task?

 b) What do I want my writing to achieve?

 c) What do I have to communicate to the audience to achieve this purpose?

2 Which of the ideas and information below would you include in your writing so that it will achieve its purpose?

- list of the dangers of smoking
- reasons why some teenagers think smoking is cool
- facts and statistics on the number of underage smokers
- advice on how to avoid peer pressure to smoke
- evidence of the damage smoking does to young lungs

Writers use a variety of **language features**, such as facts, opinions and descriptive language, to help their text achieve its purpose.

Here are some features that could be used in a text whose purpose is to argue:

facts/ evidence	questions	opinions (often stated as fact)	arguments for	arguments against

Look at how the writer of the text below uses these language features to argue that capital punishment is wrong:

Opinion stated as fact →

Capital punishment is wrong and the majority of the world's countries have recognised this. However, five countries still carry out 93% of all known executions. They are: China, Iran, Saudi Arabia, Pakistan and the USA. In the 21st century, should nations still be allowed to murder their people?

← Facts/evidence

← Question to make reader think

Argument for capital punishment →

People argue that the death penalty gives justice; if someone has committed murder then their life should be taken in return. However, most murderers spend years experiencing mental and emotional torture waiting to find out whether their death sentence will be carried out. Murderers who snapped and killed in a moment of passion suffer far more waiting for their execution than their victims ever did.

← Argument against it

ResultsPlus Controlled assessment tip

▲ When you study the task you have been given for your controlled assessment, think:
- What do I want my writing to achieve?
- What do I have to communicate to the audience to achieve this purpose?

ACTIVITY 2

Read Text A below and Texts B and C on page 59.

1 Match each of the purposes in the box below to their correct text: Text A, Text B or Text C.

persuade	inform	argue

2 Which of the following features are used in each text? Copy and complete this chart.

Feature	Text A	Text B	Text C
points that show the writer's views are sensible		✓	
reasons against the opposite point of view			
evidence			
examples			
opinions			
questions			

3 For each text write a sentence about each feature you have identified, saying how it helps the text to achieve its purpose. You could start like this:

The opinions tell readers what the writer thinks is good about …

4 What features would you include in each of the following texts?

a) a podcast that explains the work done by firefighters

b) a website giving reviews of mobile phones

c) an advertisement persuading readers to donate money to your favourite charity

Text A

NAKEDDESIRE

Honda's range of Naked motorcycles is a glorious celebration of all that's best in basic day-to-day biking. Ranging from urban icons through friendly playmates to all-out hell-raisers, they offer versatile power, reliable performance and exquisite styling. And now with 0% finance* available on selected models they have never been more desirable.

Text B

END FACTORY FARMING

home • help • donate • go veg

Most of Britain's eggs are produced on battery farms, where hens are squashed together in small cages. They can never spread their wings, scratch in the earth, perch or make a nest, dust-bathe, search for food that is tasty and natural or even walk or run. Can this be considered to be a fair life?

Text C

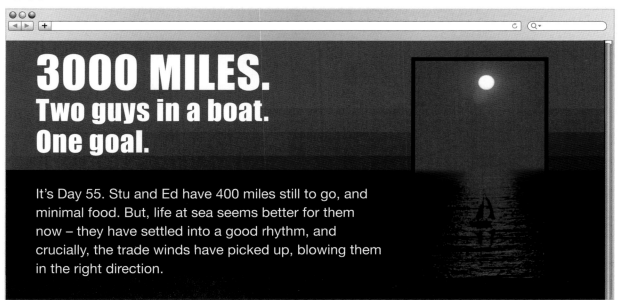

3000 MILES.
Two guys in a boat.
One goal.

It's Day 55. Stu and Ed have 400 miles still to go, and minimal food. But, life at sea seems better for them now – they have settled into a good rhythm, and crucially, the trade winds have picked up, blowing them in the right direction.

ACTIVITY 3

Read the following task:

Write an article for your school or college newspaper in which you review a new cafe that has opened in your area.

1 What is the purpose of this task?

2 What features would you include in your response to this task?

3 Write the first two paragraphs of your response to this task.

2 Audience

When you know who your **audience** is, you can decide what your readers will be interested in. You can work out what your audience needs by following these steps:

First read the brief for your task. Who is the *audience* that you have to write for? What **content** do you have to write about? For example:

> Write a magazine article *for young women* encouraging them to **take more exercise.**

Next think about what people in your audience are like and how they live.

A young woman might be a 20-year-old girl. She probably hasn't got much spare cash. She might enjoy going clubbing with her friends.

Then ask yourself what kinds of exercise would suit the people you described and the way they live.

Exercise that would suit a 20-year-old girl would need to be quite cheap, and it would be good if she could do it with her friends. She might consider swimming, dancing or using a fitness DVD.

ACTIVITY 1

Imagine you had to write a leaflet persuading people to take more exercise.

1 What sort of exercise would be likely to suit the following people? Complete a copy of the chart.

Audience	What kind of exercise would this audience be interested in?
A 12-year-old boy living in a big city where there are lots of facilities.	
An overweight 40-year-old man who works long hours in an office.	
An older couple who have retired to the countryside.	

ACTIVITY 2

Read the following task.

> Write a leaflet advising parents how to help their child through the difficult teenage years.

1 Who is the audience?

2 What kinds of thing will interest this audience? You could think about:
- what teenagers need from their parents
- how to help teenagers make good choices
- how to work through issues like money, staying out later, etc.
- any other aspects of this topic.

This is part of what one student, Jo, wrote in response to the task.

Needs to give ideas about how to work through these issues

Life is really tough being a teenager with nagging parents. My mum just goes on and on and on all the time about what I wear, what time I got in last night, who was I with?... It's sooo boring. I can't wait to leave home!

Says what her mum shouldn't do, not what she should

Needs to give solutions

I never have enough money. My mum smokes. I think if she'd just stop then all the money she spends on cigarettes she could give to me and then I'd be able to buy some nice clothes. There's this really nice top I've seen but all we do is row when I ask her for the money to buy it.

Needs to give ideas how to work through these issues

I think I already make good choices — I don't smoke so I'm making a better choice than my Mum.

Doesn't say how parents can help teenagers make good choices

ACTIVITY 3

1 Use the comments on Jo's text to rewrite her response so that it is more suitable for the audience.

ACTIVITY 4

Study the brief you have been given for your controlled assessment task or one of the practice controlled assessment tasks on page 85. Copy and complete the chart below.

1 Who is your audience?

2 What will interest them about the content you have to write about?

Audience	What would they be interested in?

3 Formal and informal language

This lesson will help you to...

* understand how to write for the audience and purpose of your task

Knowing the audience and purpose for your task will help you work out how formal your writing should be.

- Your writing should be **formal** if you are writing for an **official audience**, like a letter to your headmaster.
- You can use **informal** writing if you are writing to a **familiar or casual audience**, like a website for teenagers.

Look at the two emails below. They are on the same topic but use different language features, which have been highlighted. Text A is a teacher writing to a student; Text B is the same student writing to a friend.

Read the two emails and the notes on why Text A is formal and Text B is informal.

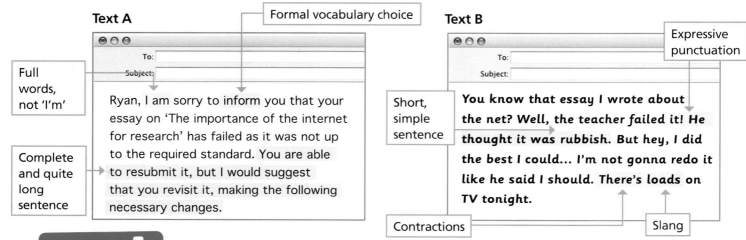

Text A

Formal vocabulary choice

Full words, not 'I'm'

Complete and quite long sentence

To:
Subject:

Ryan, I am sorry to inform you that your essay on 'The importance of the internet for research' has failed as it was not up to the required standard. You are able to resubmit it, but I would suggest that you revisit it, making the following necessary changes.

Text B

Expressive punctuation

Short, simple sentence

To:
Subject:

You know that essay I wrote about the net? Well, the teacher failed it! He thought it was rubbish. But hey, I did the best I could... I'm not gonna redo it like he said I should. There's loads on TV tonight.

Contractions

Slang

ACTIVITY 1

1 Match each of the sentences below to the correct audience.

Sentences	Audiences
A. What are your top tips for becoming a 'pro' footballer?	Children at an after school club
B. It has come to our attention that team members are not wearing the correct Olympic Games uniform.	Teenagers speaking to an adult
C. In another spot was Dappy – right in the middle of loads of giant blue Adidas bags stuffed with sneakers and clothing – trying to match a red tracky with red kicks.	Adults in an official situation

2 Make a note of any language features in the sentences that helped you decide. Copy and complete these sentences.

Sentence A language features include: ...

Sentence B language features include: ...

Sentence C language features include: ...

ACTIVITY 2

1 Read the following task.

> Write an article for a magazine for parents arguing for or against making school students do some exercise for 30 minutes each day.

a) Who is the audience?

b) How formal or informal should the writing be?

2 Read Sunita's response to the task. The highlighted words show you two examples of Sunita's writing being too informal for the task.

a) List **five** ways Sunita can make the language she used suit the audience better.

b) Rewrite Sunita's letter in more formal language.

Some students just get mardy at the thought of taking any exercise. But if you don't do any exercise when you're at school and spend all your time guzzling and studying (or not) then you won't do any different when you leave school.

Perhaps you'll have a longer and happier life if you get into some good habits while you're younger. Thirty minutes each day isn't long. Schools could just set up games of footie, or take kids for a run or set up an aerobics or dance class. It doesn't have to cost a lot.

ResultsPlus Watch out!

■ Don't use text speak or swearing in your writing. The audience might be your friends or people who are the same age as you, so you might think that you should write in this way. However, you are trying to show you are good at English, so you have to show you can use proper words and sentences.

4 Form

This lesson will help you to...

* understand how to use the correct form for your task

* use the form to help you decide what to include and how to write your text

The brief for your controlled assessment task will tell you what **form** to write your text in.

Examples of forms you might be asked to write in include:

* a script for a podcast

* a webpage

* a newspaper article.

Each form has a set of features which you should include in your writing. Studying examples of the form you have to write in will help you work out what features you should include in your text.

Look at the following leaflet. Some typical features of this form have been pointed out.

← main heading

WHAT'S WRONG WITH CRATING?

subheadings →

paragraphs →

* **No, a crate will not help a puppy learn to "hold it."** Puppies' bladders are not fully developed until they are 4 to 6 months old, so trying to force them to learn something that they are incapable of learning can backfire.

* **No, crates do not promote a feeling of security.** On the contrary, many dogs who are "crate trained" for long periods develop separation anxiety, depression, hyperactivity, and other types of anti-social behavior.

* **No, he doesn't "love" his crate.** He loves YOU. And he'll do anything to please you, including sitting behind bars, waiting patiently for you to free him.

* **No, a crate is not similar to a playpen, crib, or den.** A crate is a cramped, impoverished environment that prevents dogs from engaging in basic normal activities, such as looking out the window, walking around, and stretching out comfortably.

Using an exercise pen, gating off a puppy-proofed room, tethering your puppy to you, making arrangements with a dog walker during the day, putting in a doggie door, going home at lunchtime and not working late, providing interactive toys (such as Kongs), and deciding that your couch isn't more important than your relationship with your dog are all better options than a crate. But mostly, puppies and dogs just need consistent, attentive, knowledgeable training and care—just as children do—not warehousing in a crate.

← informal language

No more denial! A crate is nothing more than a convenience device for busy humans—but it's not good for your dog. No animal on the face of the Earth "loves" being locked inside a cage, including your dog. If you still doubt it, go on—lock yourself inside a crate and see what you think.

For more information, visit **HelpingAnimals.com**

ACTIVITY 1

Study Texts A and B below and Texts C and D on page 66.

1 Decide which of the following forms each text is written in.

| a webpage | script for a podcast | online review | speech |

2 For each form, list the features used from the list below.

a) webpage

b) script for a podcast

c) online review

d) speech

headline	informal language	subheadings
facts	interviews	paragraphs
opinions	formal language	questions

Text A

You see recycling everywhere. But does it work? The basic principle of recycling is sound enough: 'If we all recycle,' they say, 'we'll take pressure off the planet, and we'll save our money, our health and our environment.' But when you get down to the specifics, it's not always clear if we're making the savings or not. In fact we even hear that it may all be a waste of time. So what's the truth? Is recycling worth it?

Text B

AROUND THE WORLD AT 3MPH

SEEKING PHYSICAL AND EMOTIONAL CHALLENGES WHILE CIRCUMNAVIGATING THE GLOBE FOR 20 MONTHS. WE WILL BE USING AS MANY MODES OF TRANSPORT AS POSSIBLE, WITH THE EXCEPTION OF FLYING. DEPARTURE: SUNDAY, SEPTEMBER 14TH 2008

THE PLANNED ROUTE (CLICK TO ENLARGE)

WHERE WE ARE: 10TH MARCH

WEDNESDAY, MARCH 10, 2010

Colder, harder and more brutal

The moment of stepping on the train in Beijing was momentous. It was the moment where we recrossed our path from September last year and started making progress towards Hyde Park again. There would be no more weaving back and forth round the deserts

Просмотреть Around the world without flying на карте большего размера

ResultsPlus Watch out!

You do not get marks for drawing pictures, and it is not a good idea to write in columns. The examiner is interested in seeing if the words and sentences you use are **well-chosen** for the form given in the task.

Text C

[Sound of waves crashing as Presenter speaks]

Presenter: 3000 miles. 2 guys in a wooden boat. One goal. One goal. One goal.

[end of background noise] In a 24 foot plywood boat with only 2 oars to propel them and the power in their bodies to drive them on. Stuart Turnbull and Edward Bayliss will row unsupported across the Atlantic Ocean in aid of Cancer Research UK [single crash of waves followed by a few seconds of theme music which then fades to background]

Presenter: Hello and welcome to this the long anticipated final instalment of the Atlantic 06 podcast. During the last four months we have been reporting on the story of Ed Bayliss and Stu Turnbull as they row the Atlantic Ocean in aid of Cancer Research UK. It's been a life changing experience for the two boys and we've covered it all…

Text D

GREATEST MOVIE SEQUELS

HOME / NEWS / LINKS / TOP-TEN

SHREK 2

Why's it so good? Three words: Puss. In. Boots. He's adorable, he's deadly and he goes nuts for catnip. The interplay between Puss and Donkey has become the principal reason to watch the series ("The position of annoying talking sidekick has already been taken!"), while Shrek and Fiona are reduced to playing straight men in the foreground.

How does it stack up to the original? It's not as good: there are far too many characters, the plot, similarly, is needlessly overcomplicated, and even Puss can't make up for the lack of a great villain (much as we enjoyed Everett's Charming). And while some of the endless movie referencing works well ("Be gooooood"), there's so much of it that it becomes exhausting.

Glaring error: The practice of inserting celebrity cameos, and then redubbing with locals in other territories, started here and it's wildly annoying. Kate Thornton for Joan Rivers? Outrageous!

ACTIVITY 2

Read the following task:

> Write a blog entry for a sports fan website in which you review a recent sporting event.

1 What features should the text use? Look back to the table of features on page 65 (Activity 1, question 2) to help you.

2 Write the first two paragraphs of the blog entry.

ResultsPlus Self assessment

Check your answer to **Activity 2**. Have you:
• selected words and sentences that show a clear sense of the **audience** and **purpose**?
• selected words and sentences that link to the **form**?

Here is an example of a controlled assessment task you could be expected to answer.

In your response to this task you would be expected to write using the conventions, or features, of an article.

Write an article for your school magazine in which you explain why school is important to you.

(20 marks)

ACTIVITY 3

Write the opening two paragraphs of the article explaining why school is important to you. You should focus on using the right features of an article.

You should spend 20 minutes on this task.

Results Plus Self assessment

Before you complete this self-assessment activity you might like to read some sample answers to this task on the following pages (68 – 69).

Check your answer to Activity 3:
- Did you include a headline for your article?
- Did you give all the **background details** for your article in the opening paragraph?
- Did you use a **variety of sentences**, like a question, short sentences, sentences with connectives, that are common in articles?

Maximise your marks

Write the opening two paragraphs of the article explaining why school is important to you. You should focus on using the right features of an article.

Here are three student answers to the article task on page 67. Around and after the answers are examiner comments. Read both the student answers and examiner comments. Then complete the activity at the bottom of page 69.

Student 1 – Extract typical of a grade E answer

A simple grasp of the idea of the article but the informal language isn't really appropriate

> I guess school is important in some ways cause they prepare you for stuff later on and they make it so that you can go onto college and do what you like then. The teachers always say in assemblies that it is about opening doors and things like that. I think it is more to do with the fact that you get to have a great time with your mates and you occasionally do a bit of the work that the teachers force you to do.

No change in paragraph

Examiner summary

This part of the answer is typical of grade E performance. The student has included some details that might be seen as appropriate in an article, such as mentioning the school assembly and the idea that teachers give. However, the lack of paragraphs and the informal language show that the student only has a basic grasp of the rules of an article.

Student 2 – Extract typical of a grade D answer

This is an appropriate start to an article as it introduces the reader to the topic

> School is important to me because I want to do well later in life and I want to make sure that I earn enough to look after me and my family and the people around me. I think it is important that I work hard for my exams and that I do other stuff that will look good on my CV.
>
> I think school is important too because it means I get to meet up with my friends and we can have time to get to know each and sometimes have fun.

Sentences are fairly accurate but there is over use of 'I think' at the beginning of sentences

The student is trying to keep the feel of an article but the repetition of 'I think' means this doesn't always feel like the appropriate tone

Examiner summary

This part of the answer is typical of grade D performance. The student has done well to use a topic sentence at the beginning of each paragraph, which is typical of a newspaper article. The sentences and word choice show that the student is able to make some accurate choices but they tend to be repetitive. The use of 'I think' repeatedly makes the tone seem too personal for a newspaper article, even one intended for a school magazine.

'We' is a good selection of word as it gives the article more authority

The first paragraph introduces the topic and this topic sentence shows the student is developing the idea

School: What's the point?

We attend school every day from early in the morning through to late afternoon. We spend more time with our teachers than we do with our parents in term time! Is it really worth the hassle?

The obvious answer is yes, school is very important. We work hard at school and then we get good grades. There are lots of things that we need to learn that will help us become successful in later life. We will earn more money and we will be able to find lots of ways to make ourselves happy.

Some evidence of control over sentences

Examiner summary

This part of the answer is typical of grade C performance. The use of 'we' is a good word choice because it makes the article sound like it has a lot more authority. The use of an exclamation and a question adds some evidence of control to the article and helps to introduce the issue in an interesting way. The second paragraph becomes a little more repetitive but the student has developed an idea appropriately from a topic sentence.

ResultsPlus
Build better answers

Move from a Grade **E** to Grade **D**
You need to make sure that you change paragraph when you introduce a new idea. You also need to show that you can select the appropriate level of language. This is clear in the difference between Student 1 and Student 2. Student 1 uses informal language and forgets to change paragraph. Student 2 remembers to use a topic sentence at the beginning of paragraphs that clearly separates their appropriate ideas.

Move from a Grade **D** to Grade **C**
In this part of your task you need to think about the tone you need to create. Student 3 chose 'we' while Student 2 chose 'I'. This small difference makes Student 3 sound more of an authority in the article, like it is something that you would read in a newspaper. Student 3 also develops the idea in the second paragraph rather than starting a new idea.

PUTTING IT INTO PRACTICE

1 Write the opening two paragraphs of a blog about your school day. Use the sentence starters to help you practise beginning new paragraphs.

Another day at school has flown by ...

Obviously Art was the best thing about today ...

5 Generating ideas

This lesson will help you to...

* create appropriate and engaging ideas for your writing

* make sure you have enough to write about

You will be given a brief for your controlled assessment writing task that will tell you what to write. It will look something like this:

> Write a script for a podcast for a teenage website in which you describe your favourite film.

When you are given a writing brief you need to work out:

* **WHAT** – what the **content** of your text should be (what you have to write about)

* **WHO** – what kind of **audience** you are writing for (for example, teenagers, football fans)

* **WHY** – what the **purpose** of your writing should be (for example, to persuade, to inform)

* **HOW** – what **form** you need to write it in (for example, an article, a podcast).

Use the questions below to help you find out what you need to know.

Audience: *WHO* am I writing for?
Teenagers who like films and visit websites – so they'll be aged between 8 and 12

Purpose: *WHY* am I writing the text?
To describe the film and tell the teenagers what makes it such a good film.

Content: *WHAT* do I have to write about?
My favourite film. That's Quantum of Solace – it's a James Bond film.

> Write a script for a podcast for a teenage website in which you describe your favourite film.

Form: *HOW* do I have to write the text?
As a script for a podcast

ACTIVITY 1

Study the brief you have been given for your controlled assessment writing task or one of the practice controlled assessment tasks on page 85.

1 Complete a chart like the one below showing **what** you have to write the text about, **who** you have to write it for, **why** you have to write it and **how** you have to write it.

Content (What)	Audience (Who)	Purpose (Why)	Form (How)

You need to make sure you have enough good ideas to write about. One way you can think up lots of ideas is by making a spider diagram.

First put the subject you are writing about in a circle in the middle of a clean page.

Next jot down your main ideas around the circle.

Then work on each main idea. Note down what other points or details you could write about it.

As you create your spider diagram keep asking yourself: *What other ideas or information would fit in with what I have to write about? What else would be interesting for my readers to know?*

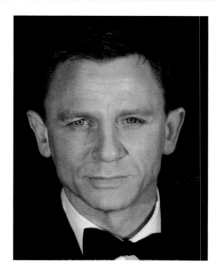

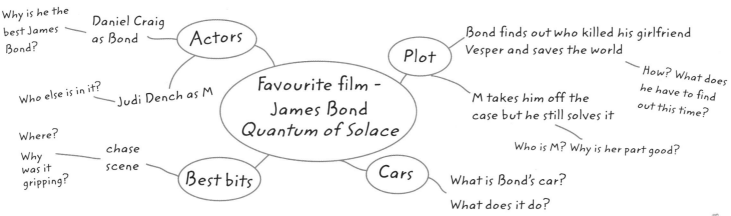

You may need more information before you can begin to write. Use your preparation time to do some research. Look for the answers in books, newspapers or magazines, on the internet, or by asking your family or experts on the subject.

ACTIVITY 2

Study the brief you have been given for your controlled assessment writing task or one of the practice controlled assessment tasks on page 85.

1 Make a spider diagram for the brief you have been given.

    a) Start by jotting down your main ideas.

    b) Add any other information to build on each idea.

2 Highlight in a different colour any information in your spider diagram that you need to research.

3 Work out how you can find each piece of information you need. Will you use books, newspapers, magazines, internet, family, friends or experts?

6 Organising and linking paragraphs

This lesson will help you to...

* organise your ideas within paragraphs
* make links between your paragraphs

You need to write in **paragraphs**. Each paragraph should begin with a different main point which you then explain in more detail. It is easier to write in paragraphs if you plan them first.

First list your main points in the order you will write about them.

Next note down the smaller points, details and evidence that you want to put in each paragraph.

Then note down any words or phrases you want to use when you are writing each paragraph.

You can make your notes in a chart like this:

Main point	Details	Words or phrases to use
It's fun to go out with friends but keep safe	• Describe excitement of getting ready at start of evening • Describe the end of evening and the worst situation – last bus gone – having to walk home down cold, dark, lonely alley – scared and then being followed...	Because... Footsteps behind me? Am I being followed?
Get home safely	• Find out the time of the last bus or train home • Agree who you are going to travel home with • If someone is going to pick you up agree when and where – make sure it's brightly lit and safe to walk to	

ACTIVITY 1

1 Look at the controlled assessment writing task you started planning for in Lesson 5, Activity 2 (page 71). Make a paragraph plan for your response to this task. Model it on the chart above.

Main point	Details	Words or phrases to use

You need to use **connectives** or linking words to join each paragraph to the one before it. These words act like signposts telling your reader what direction the text is going in. They can achieve different purposes, as the chart below shows.

Purpose	Connective	Example
to **order** events	next, then, since	*Decide how you are going to get home.* **Then** *get ready to go out.*
to **order** points	firstly, finally	**First of all** *make sure you know the time of the last bus home.*
to **add** points	also, in addition, similarly	*Not knowing how you'll get home is stupid;* **also** *it leaves you in danger.*
to **argue against** points	but, however, although	**Although** *most people are good people, you can't be sure that someone you've just met is a safe person to take you home.*
to **explain** points	because, therefore, so, then, for example	**For example**, *you might be safer sharing a taxi back* **because** *it will drop you off at your home* **so then** *you don't have to walk back alone from the bus stop.*

ACTIVITY 2

Look at the paragraph plan you made in Activity 1 and the chart above.

1 Write three of the paragraphs from the plan you made in Activity 1. Use the chart to help you choose the best connectives to link points within and between paragraphs in your writing task. Challenge yourself to use some new connectives.

ResultsPlus Controlled assessment tip

What if you have finished your writing and you have forgotten to include paragraphs? The best thing to do is to go through and put this mark // where you think a paragraph should be. You do not have to write everything out again!

7 Organising your writing

* structure your writing with a clear and effective beginning, middle and end

* choose the best order to write about your points

You need to **organise** your paragraphs so that your writing has a clear beginning, middle and end. This will make it flow well for your reader and help them to follow what you have written. It will also help your writing to achieve its purpose.

The **beginning** of a text has to do **three** things:

- Grab your reader's attention.
- Give enough background information for the reader to be able to understand the text.
- Introduce the main idea that your text is about.

ACTIVITY 1

Look at the six key points below. These are the points that one student, Jack, wants to write about in order to persuade people to give up smoking.

- Smoking wastes your money.
- Smoking causes many problems.
- Smoking makes your breath and clothes smell. It stains your home.
- Smoking kills you — the diseases it causes are really painful and a frightening way to die.
- Smokers would live longer, fitter lives if they stopped.
- The National Health Service would save lots of money by not having to treat smoking-related diseases. Everyone could pay less tax.

1 What is the main idea Jack should use for his introduction?

2 Which of the points above will grab readers' attention and give them enough background information?

ACTIVITY 2

Read the following task.

> Write a blog for your school's website in which you comment on the importance of friendship.

1 List six key points you would want to make when writing this task.

2 What is the main idea you should write about in your introduction?

3 Write an introduction to this task.

You then need to work out the best order to write the points for the **middle** part of your text.

- Put them in the best order to achieve your purpose. For example, an argument would give reasons for and then against each point.

- Group similar ideas together. This makes it easy for your reader to follow your text.

- Make sure you save a strong point to end your text.

This is how Jack decides to order his points:

1. Smoking kills you — the diseases it causes are really painful and a frightening way to die.

2. Smokers would live longer, fitter lives if they stopped.

3. Smoking wastes your money.

4. Smoking makes your breath and clothes smell. It stains your home.

5. The National Health Service would save lots of money by not having to treat smoking-related diseases. Everyone could pay less tax.

The **last** paragraph of a text should do these **two** things:

- Make sure the text achieves its purpose. You may need to tell the audience what their response should be or remind them what they have gained by reading your text.

- Be memorable. Leave your readers with something to think about or remember.

This is Jack's ending:

Stop smoking before it ruins your life, empties your wallet and makes the country bankrupt.

ACTIVITY 3

Go back to the key points you created in Activity 2.

1 What is the best order in which to write your points?

2 Write the middle and final paragraphs of your blog. Make sure you keep your writing because you will need it again later in this unit.

ResultsPlus Watch out!

■ When you write the introduction to your text in your controlled assessment, make sure it:
- grabs the reader's attention
- gives enough background information
- introduces the main idea of the text.

8 Crafting vocabulary

This lesson will help you to...

* make appropriate and effective vocabulary choices

You need to choose the best words to suit your audience when you write. You have already looked at formal and informal writing in Lesson 3. You also need to think about the **vocabulary** you use. For example:

* You need to choose simpler words if you are writing for children than you would use for an adult.

* Experts are happy to read technical words but a general audience may not understand them.

Compare Texts A and B below. Text A is written for a general audience, and Text B is written for teenagers. Notice the vocabulary used for different audiences.

Text A

If you are interested in film-making then take a look at **Paper Mannequin Productions** website. They are award winning makers of films with a relevant social or political message e.g. If Not Now, When? which is about the effect of teenage knife crime. On the website you can view their films and give your thoughts and feedback. You can also find out about new projects and how recent films are doing.

The highlighted words are examples of everyday vocabulary, like you might hear on the news – no slang or informal words or phrases.

Text B

It's Friday night? Bored of the same old dinner and a movie? Well grab your mates. Get your socks. It's time… for bowling!
I know what you're thinking – bowling is totally naff. But think again! There are loads of new bowling alleys opening up: ones that actually play good music and have great food. You can just have a laugh by doing stuff like bowling through your legs or you can get competitive and brag about your four strikes! So Google a bowling alley near you and check it out!

Here the highlighted words are examples of vocabulary choices aimed at a teenage audience – slang and young phrases are used.

ACTIVITY 1

1 Rewrite Text B by changing the highlighted phrases to suit a general audience, like readers of a magazine article. Use a dictionary and thesaurus to find alternative vocabulary.

2 Rewrite Text A to suit a teenage audience, like listeners to a school podcast.

ResultsPlus Watch out!

■ You get more credit for using appropriate vocabulary than you do for spelling. Don't avoid using words because you think they are too difficult to spell.

The Writing Task for the student

Complete one task from those below.

EITHER

Write an article for a magazine in which you persuade readers about an environmental issue from a specific point of view. (20)

OR

Write the script for a podcast for a website aimed at young people aged 11–14, where you inform them about an environmental issue. (20)

Examiner's tip

Pick one task here. Remember to make your response appropriate for the given audience, purpose and form.

Unit 2 The Writer's Craft The Writer's Voice

This unit will help you to prepare for the writing task in your examination (Section B in English Language and Section C in English). This examination writing task will ask you to write a response to a situation, issue or problem. You will need to write about your views and opinions, and you will need to use evidence to support these views and opinions.

This section of the book will help you to build on the writing skills you developed in Unit 1. It will give you plenty of strategies for writing effectively under a time limit in an exam. It will also explore different ways that you can approach the writing task.

The activities you'll complete in this unit are all focused on helping you to achieve the best grade you can in this section of the examination.

Your assessment

Unit 2 is an examination unit. The first part of your examination will focus on the set texts you have studied in class, and the final section will be a writing task, which is the focus of this unit of the book. You will have to answer **one** question from a choice of **two**.

Your response to the writing section must show that you can:

✔ reflect on ideas, issues, experiences and events, rather than writing a narrative or description

✔ write in a form, such as a newspaper article, formal report or magazine review, targeting a specified audience

✔ reflect and comment on contemporary issues, situations or problems that are relevant to you, such as lifestyle, school or college life, local issues or national issues that affect young people.

Assessment Objectives

Your Unit 2 examination will be based on how well you:

✔ Write clearly using forms and appropriate vocabulary.

✔ Organise information and ideas.

✔ Use a range of sentence structures, with accurate punctuation and spelling.

This student book unit will help you to understand how to do this so that you can write a successful response in the examination.

1 Purpose

This lesson will help you to...

* understand *what* and *how* to write for different purposes

In your examination you will be given a choice of two writing tasks. If you are taking the Foundation Tier paper they will look something like this:

> Write a magazine article arguing for or against the following statement: 'Mobile phones should be banned in schools'. In your article you may wish to consider:
>
> * the effect texting has on students' writing and language skills
> * the distraction mobiles cause in classrooms
> * peer pressure to have mobile phones
> * the possibility of using mobile phones to cheat
> * any other aspects of this topic.

You need to work out what **purpose** you are being asked to write for. You can identify the purpose by searching the task for key words that show what the readers will get from the text. For example:

> Write a magazine article **arguing** for or against the following statement: 'Mobile phones should be banned in schools'.

The word in **bold** type tells you that you need to write a text that is an argument. Look for key words like this in your writing tasks.

ACTIVITY 1

Read the three writing tasks below.

1 For each task:

a) pick out the key words that show you what the reader will get from the text

b) make a note of what the text's purpose is.

> **A:** Should parents be banned from smacking their own children? Write a letter to your MP arguing your point of view for or against the ban.

Key words: ...

Purpose: ...

> **B:** Write an article for a young person's magazine discussing the advantages and disadvantages of starting the school day at 8 a.m.

Key words: ...

Purpose: ...

> **C:** Your local council is planning some changes and has asked you to write a review of community facilities for young people and suggestions for future improvements.

Key words: ...

Purpose: ...

Once you know what purpose you have to write for, you can decide **how** to write your text so that it will achieve that purpose.

ACTIVITY 2

Study Texts A to D on pages 89–91. Each is an extract of a text that has a different purpose. The features you should use to achieve that purpose are listed next to each text.

1 Find examples of the features being used in each text. Make a chart like this for each text to record your answers.

Features of ... an explanation text	Examples in ... Text A
Tell your reader how and why	you can get the flu from someone's sneeze or by touching your nose or eyes after being around someone with the flu because the virus is spread through infected droplets
Organise points in a clear logical order	
Give reasons and explain them fully	
See all sides of an issue	

Text A: Explain

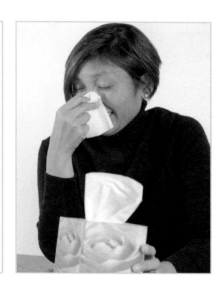

How flu is spread

If someone already has flu their sneeze can travel the length of a bus or tube carriage. If you are travelling with them then you will have inhaled infected droplets. The virus has got past your body's first line of defence – the hairs and mucus in the nose, which traps them. You could also let the virus into your body by touching your nose or eyes after being in contact with someone with a cold or flu. Once it is inside your body the virus takes over your cells and uses them to reproduce by the million.

When you write a text to **explain** you should:

- tell your reader how and why
- organise your points in a clear logical order
- give reasons and explain them fully
- see all sides of an issue.

Text B: Persuade

RAISE MONEY FOR CHARITY

PARACHUTING

Imagine standing at the edge of an open doorway in an aircraft flying at 10,000 feet, then jumping out and free-falling at over 120mph. Always wanted to do it? Now's your chance.

All jumps take place at centres approved by the British Parachute Association with full training provided on the day or on the weekend of your jump.

WHAT YOU NEED TO DO

All you need to do is raise a minimum of £395 – £535 in sponsorship (depending on the type of jump and where you do it) and you're flying...literally. Raise the minimum amount of sponsorship and you can jump for free.

Do a Tandem Skydive and you will be freefalling through the air (without the parachute deployed) for several thousand feet. You will be harnessed to a professional parachute instructor at all times throughout the descent.

This is the only way you can jump from such an altitude without spending thousands of pounds becoming a free-fall parachutist. It is literally the chance of a lifetime!

© Shelter 2010

When you write a text to **persuade** you should:

- build your points to a conclusion
- make it clear what you want your audience to do
- give examples, opinions, facts, reasons, evidence
- sometimes speak directly to your reader
- use emotive language to sway your reader's feelings
- use questions and persuasive words.

Text C: Argue

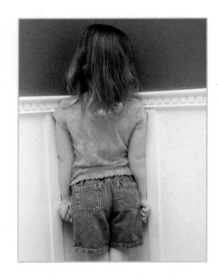

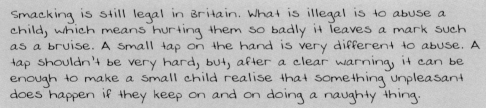

Smacking is still legal in Britain. What is illegal is to abuse a child, which means hurting them so badly it leaves a mark such as a bruise. A small tap on the hand is very different to abuse. A tap shouldn't be very hard, but, after a clear warning, it can be enough to make a small child realise that something unpleasant does happen if they keep on and on doing a naughty thing.

Some people think smacking should be banned altogether. The NSPCC's Full Stop campaign calls for a total ban on any physical punishments. However, the alternatives to smacking are often unrealistic. TV programmes like Supernanny suggest putting a child on a naughty step, but that means that you have to be somewhere where you can leave your child on one. It's not easy in a supermarket. It also means everything has to wait for the child to get sorted. Other children have to wait for their playmate to come back to the game and so they end up being punished too. But a smack is quick and over in a moment.

When you write to **argue** you should:

- make reasonable, sensible points
- organise your points so that they build your case
- either give both sides of the argument or be one-sided (depending on the task)
- give opinions, reasons and evidence.

Text D: Comment

Again and again, the public have made their feelings crystal clear about fortnightly rubbish collections and hefty fines for putting refuse in the 'wrong' bin: they don't like them.

Yet, undeterred, politicians impose ever-more irksome and unhygienic rules.

Under the latest plans, every home in the country will be forced to throw waste food into a kitchen slop bucket – with yet more fines for those who disobey.

This will make precious little difference to the future of the planet.

But it's good news for rats.

When you write a text to **comment** on an issue you should:

• give a well thought through assessment of a topic, issue or item

• break your topic down into its key parts and cover each one in a clear, sensible order

• give your opinions and back them up with facts, reasons and evidence

• use emotive language to stir readers' feelings.

ACTIVITY 3

1 Read the two writing tasks below. Write down the purpose of and features for each task.

> **A:** Write a magazine article arguing whether fashion magazines and advertisements should use very thin models.

> **B:** Write a letter to your local newspaper commenting that teenagers have a bad image that ignores the many positive things that they do.

2 Here is part of one student's response to Task B. Identify how he could change it so that it would achieve its purpose better.

> I think it is dreadful that some teenagers give the rest of us a bad name. It's not fair because most teenagers are nice people. People only ever remember the bad things a few teenagers do.

3 Write the first two paragraphs responding to Task A. Make sure you include the features that will help your text achieve its purpose.

 Results**Plus** **Watch out!**

An argument in writing is not the same as an argument with a friend or family member. When you are writing an argument you have to be reasonable. You need to be able to see both sides of the issue. You would not get angry when writing your argument – you would calmly weigh up the different points of view.

2 Audience

You need to work out what **audience** you are being asked to write for. Identifying your audience will tell you how to write because different audiences need to know different things.

First look at the task to work out who the audience is.

> Write a speech for the end-of-year student awards discussing whether the age that students can leave education should be lowered to 14.

My audience will be the people at the awards — students, teachers and parents.

Then decide what ideas and information you should include to suit the audience. For example:

- *Teenagers might want people to know why they would like to leave school early, e.g. to get a job.*

- *Parents might want to hear about the effect this would have on families, e.g. teenagers might earn some money to contribute to the household, but they will not earn much.*

- *Teachers might want to hear about the benefits of not having students in the classroom who really do not want to be there, e.g. less disruption, able to concentrate on more advanced subjects.*

ACTIVITY 1

Look at the following writing task:

> Write a magazine article for teenagers explaining why film and game rating certificates are important. You may wish to consider:
> - the level of violence in some films and games
> - what the certificates indicate
> - any other ideas you may have.

1 Identify the audience.

2 Write down **three** ideas or pieces of information you would include to interest the audience.

ResultsPlus Watch out!

If you are asked to write for a teenage audience, you should never write very informally. Remember: you are **always** expected to write using correct grammar!

Knowing your audience and purpose helps you decide how formal your writing should be. Learn the following rules to help you work out whether you need to be **formal** or **informal** when writing:

Formal language:

- Use formal language when writing for a serious reason or for an official audience, like your boss or your head teacher.

- In formal writing, use complete sentences. Do not use abbreviations or slang.

No contractions: 'cannot' not 'can't'

formal language: 'poor' not 'bad' or 'rubbish'

No contractions: 'There is' not 'There's'

Young people cannot be blamed for the poor state of the area. There is little for them to do and nowhere else for them to meet other than the centre of town.

Informal language:

- Use informal language when your purpose is not official or when you're writing for a familiar or casual audience, like writing a letter to your friends.

- In informal writing, do not use very informal language, but you can use some abbreviations, contractions and common phrases.

Contraction

Common phrase

informal language: 'tough' not 'difficult'

Common phrase

It's not tough to keep fit and healthy and stay out of trouble if you make the most of your local leisure centre.

ACTIVITY 2

1 How formal should your writing be for this writing task? Use the rules above to help you:

Write a guide informing visitors about a place of interest that they could visit.

2 Darren wrote the following paragraph in response to the task above. Rewrite the paragraph so that it suits his audience better.

A really cool place to visit is Alton Towers. The rides there are AMAZING! There's stuff for little kids as well as older teenagers and there are lots of places to eat and chill out too. The most exciting rides at Alton Towers at the moment are the Oblivion and Submission rollercoasters. There are two other rides you shouldn't miss either — Air and Rita: Queen of Speed. For a laugh you should challenge yourself to do all four rides in a day.

3 Form

* understand the typical features used in different forms of writing

The writing task will tell you what **form** you should write your text in. These forms could include a newspaper article, blog, letter, leaflet, speech or report.

You will not be marked on how your text looks in the examination, so do not include pictures or colour, or write in columns.

The examiner is looking for the following in your writing:

- use of effective language

- awareness of audience and purpose

- use of the correct form and style of writing

- organisation and structure of your writing in paragraphs and sentences

- correct punctuation.

ACTIVITY 1

Study Texts A to F on pages 95–97. These texts show examples of different forms. The labels around the texts state the features of that form. Some labels are blank pointing out where another feature is.

1 Make a table like this to show what features are included in each of the different forms. Make sure you include the features missing from the labels:

Form	Features
Review	heading, subheading, opinions, evidence, facts
Formal report	
Speech	
Leaflet	
Formal letter	
Blog	

2 List as many similarities and differences between each of the following forms as you can.

a) a magazine article and a leaflet

    Similarities: ...

    Differences: ...

b) a letter and a speech

c) a blog and a letter

d) a report and a review

Text A: Review

Heading

Subheading

Opinions

Facts

Evidence

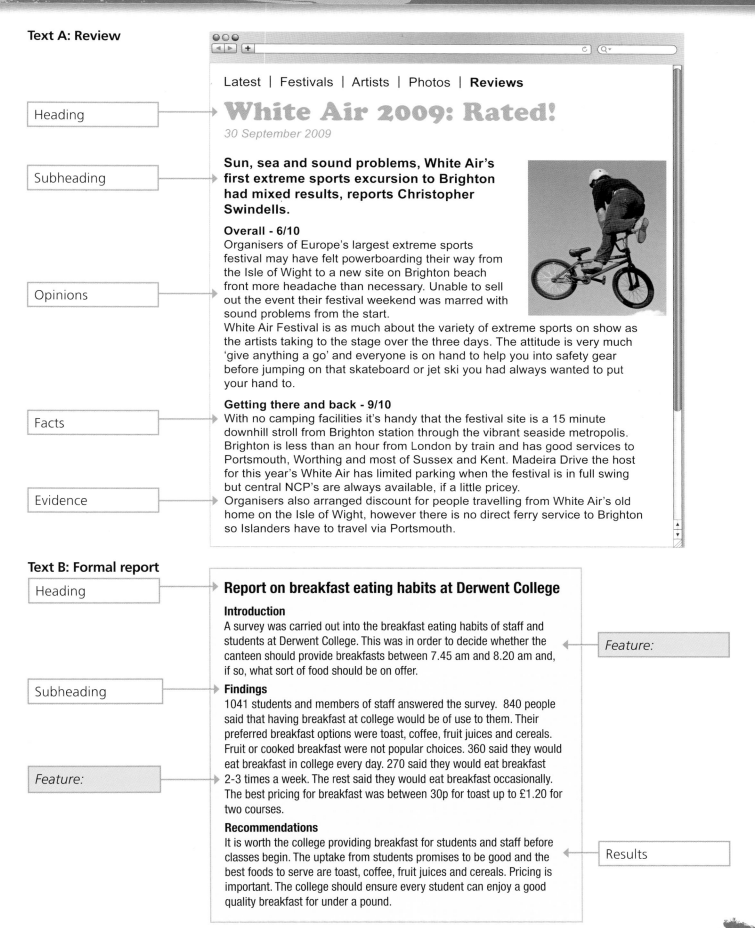

Latest | Festivals | Artists | Photos | **Reviews**

White Air 2009: Rated!

30 September 2009

Sun, sea and sound problems, White Air's first extreme sports excursion to Brighton had mixed results, reports Christopher Swindells.

Overall - 6/10
Organisers of Europe's largest extreme sports festival may have felt powerboarding their way from the Isle of Wight to a new site on Brighton beach front more headache than necessary. Unable to sell out the event their festival weekend was marred with sound problems from the start.
White Air Festival is as much about the variety of extreme sports on show as the artists taking to the stage over the three days. The attitude is very much 'give anything a go' and everyone is on hand to help you into safety gear before jumping on that skateboard or jet ski you had always wanted to put your hand to.

Getting there and back - 9/10
With no camping facilities it's handy that the festival site is a 15 minute downhill stroll from Brighton station through the vibrant seaside metropolis. Brighton is less than an hour from London by train and has good services to Portsmouth, Worthing and most of Sussex and Kent. Madeira Drive the host for this year's White Air has limited parking when the festival is in full swing but central NCP's are always available, if a little pricey.
Organisers also arranged discount for people travelling from White Air's old home on the Isle of Wight, however there is no direct ferry service to Brighton so Islanders have to travel via Portsmouth.

Text B: Formal report

Heading

Subheading

Feature:

Report on breakfast eating habits at Derwent College

Introduction
A survey was carried out into the breakfast eating habits of staff and students at Derwent College. This was in order to decide whether the canteen should provide breakfasts between 7.45 am and 8.20 am and, if so, what sort of food should be on offer.

Feature:

Findings
1041 students and members of staff answered the survey. 840 people said that having breakfast at college would be of use to them. Their preferred breakfast options were toast, coffee, fruit juices and cereals. Fruit or cooked breakfast were not popular choices. 360 said they would eat breakfast in college every day. 270 said they would eat breakfast 2-3 times a week. The rest said they would eat breakfast occasionally. The best pricing for breakfast was between 30p for toast up to £1.20 for two courses.

Recommendations
It is worth the college providing breakfast for students and staff before classes begin. The uptake from students promises to be good and the best foods to serve are toast, coffee, fruit juices and cereals. Pricing is important. The college should ensure every student can enjoy a good quality breakfast for under a pound.

Results

Text C: Speech

Greeting

Introduction

Feature:

Explain what response you want

Repetition

Prepared Remarks of President Barack Obama
Back to School Event, Arlington, Virginia, September 8, 2009

The President:

Hello everyone – how's everybody doing today? I'm here with students at Wakefield High School in Arlington, Virginia. And we've got students tuning in from all across America, kindergarten through twelfth grade. I'm glad you all could join us today.

I know that for many of you, today is the first day of school. And for those of you in kindergarten, or starting middle or high school, it's your first day in a new school, so it's understandable if you're a little nervous. I imagine there are some seniors out there who are feeling pretty good right now, with just one more year to go. And no matter what grade you're in, some of you are probably wishing it were still summer, and you could've stayed in bed just a little longer this morning.

I know that feeling. When I was young, my family lived in Indonesia for a few years, and my mother didn't have the money to send me where all the American kids went to school. So she decided to teach me extra lessons herself, Monday through Friday – at 4:30 in the morning.

Now I wasn't too happy about getting up that early. A lot of times, I'd fall asleep right there at the kitchen table. But whenever I'd complain, my mother would just give me one of those looks and say, "This is no picnic for me either, buster."

So I know some of you are still adjusting to being back at school. But I'm here today because I have something important to discuss with you. I'm here because I want to talk with you about your education and what's expected of all of you in this new school year.

Now I've given a lot of speeches about education. And I've talked a lot about responsibility.

I've talked about your teachers' responsibility for inspiring you, and pushing you to learn.

I've talked about your parents' responsibility for making sure you stay on track, and get your homework done, and don't spend every waking hour in front of the TV or with that Xbox.

I've talked a lot about your government's responsibility for setting high standards, supporting teachers and principals, and turning around schools that aren't working where students aren't getting the opportunities they deserve.

Text D: Leaflet

Heading

Feature:

Get Clued Up on Tattoos and Body-piercing

Thinking of getting a tattoo or piercing... here's what you should know before you make your mind up.

Do I really want this piercing / tattoo done?
You have thought about it carefully and yes you do want it done. **So what should you do now?**

Where should I go?
Don't go rushing in, check out a few places first. Ask around:
- Have any of your friends had a piercing or tattoo done recently?
- Are they happy with it?
- Did they have any problems?
- Would they go back to the same place if they wanted another tattoo / piercing?
- Was the studio clean?
- Did the piercer / tattooist know what they were doing?

Has the place been checked out by the Council?
If they have, they should have a registration certificate on display. A place where tattooing and body-piercing is done should have two registration certificates on display.

Trust your instincts
If you don't like what you see or hear then leave.

Subheadings

Information given in easy to find chunks, bullet points, etc.

Text E: Formal letter

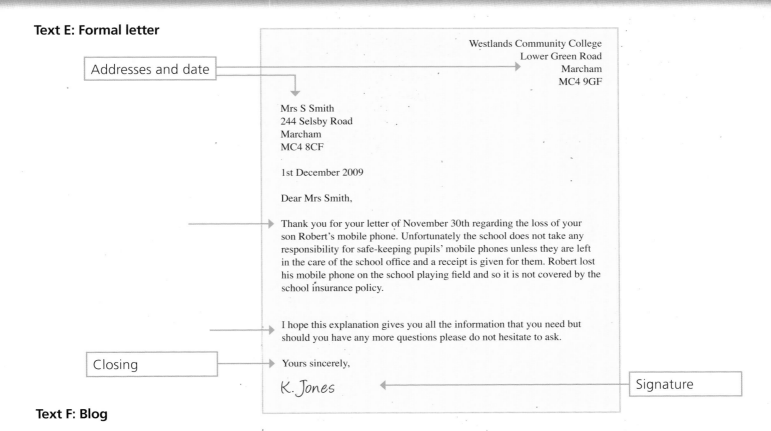

Addresses and date

Westlands Community College
Lower Green Road
Marcham
MC4 9GF

Mrs S Smith
244 Selsby Road
Marcham
MC4 8CF

1st December 2009

Dear Mrs Smith,

Thank you for your letter of November 30th regarding the loss of your son Robert's mobile phone. Unfortunately the school does not take any responsibility for safe-keeping pupils' mobile phones unless they are left in the care of the school office and a receipt is given for them. Robert lost his mobile phone on the school playing field and so it is not covered by the school insurance policy.

I hope this explanation gives you all the information that you need but should you have any more questions please do not hesitate to ask.

Closing

Yours sincerely,

K. Jones

Signature

Text F: Blog

Posted 30 September at 10.37am in the innocent foundation by Graham

4 Form in action

Knowing what features to include when writing in each form should help you work out how to write. Look at this writing task:

> Write a magazine article for parents advising how to buy good presents for teenagers.

First you should list the features of a text in the form of an article.

Then you should decide what to write about for each feature needed.

Features in an article: headlines, subheadings, paragraphs, quotations

<u>Headlines:</u> Giving great gifts to teenagers!

<u>Subheadings:</u> No more embarrassing Christmas silences, Freedom to choose

<u>Paragraphs:</u>

* **who** teenagers have strong tastes so it's best to let them choose their own things
* **what** vouchers e.g. for i tunes, Amazon, clothes, trips to cinema, favourite theme park...
* **when** birthdays, Christmas, as a thank you
* **where** buy them in stores or online
* **how** use a credit card or debit card online or in a store

<u>Quotations:</u>

* **from people with experience** e.g. teenagers describing awful presents they've been given + teenagers describing some good presents
* **from experts** e.g. parents or grandparents who have got it right

ACTIVITY 1

Look again at the writing task above.

1 Write two paragraphs of the magazine article using the plan above to help you.

ACTIVITY 2

1 What features of form would you need to include in your writing if you were given these three writing tasks?

> A: Write a speech on the topic of 'Stress and Modern Life' to be given to a group of your peers.

> B: Write a report to the school council on how well your school cares for the environment.

> C: Write a letter to an employer you would like to work for, persuading them to give you two weeks' work experience.

ACTIVITY 3

Read the following writing task:

> Write a leaflet for your school welcoming new students, giving them advice about what to expect and how to settle in easily. You may wish to include information about:
>
> * finding their way around school
> * what to do at break times, lunchtimes, etc.
> * how to get on well at school, e.g. behaviour, homework, uniform, etc.
> * anything that might be a concern to new students
> * any other aspects of this topic.

1 What form are you being asked to write in?

2 Make a list of the features you expect a text in this form to have.

William made these notes to help him respond to the task:

Notes:

- Find your way around school — get given a map on first day of term or from office, or ask other pupils.

- What to do at break times, lunchtimes etc — you can get food from the Blue Diner or you can bring a packed lunch. Go out on the field if you want to play football.

- How to get on well at school — do your homework, bring a pen to lessons, don't argue with the teachers.

- Concerns — how to make friends, are the teachers friendly, strict, etc

3 Use your list of features to plan how to structure your writing. You can use William's notes to give you some ideas about what to write.

4 Use your plan to write your text.

5 Producing ideas

Your time in the examination is short, so you need to work out **quickly** what you have to write about and how to write it. Read this writing task and use the four questions below to help you decide how to write your response:

> Write a magazine article arguing for or against the following statement: 'Mobile phones should be banned in schools'. In your article you may wish to consider:
>
> * the effect texting has on students' writing and language skills
> * the distraction mobiles cause in classrooms
> * peer pressure to have a mobile phone
> * the possibility of cheating using a mobile phone
> * any other aspects of this topic.

* **WHAT** – **What do I need to write about?**

  Should mobile phones be banned?

  Ideas: the effect on students' writing, language skills and health, peer pressure...

* **WHO** – **Who am I writing for?**

  It doesn't say, so I assume it's a general adult audience.

* **WHY** – **What is the purpose of my text?**

  To argue for or against banning mobiles — so I have to decide on my opinion and stick to it.

* **HOW** – **What form do I have to write in?**

  A magazine article.

ACTIVITY 1

Read the following writing task:

> Write a report for your school council on ways for your school to be at the heart of your local community. You may include:
>
> * a brief description of your local community and their needs
> * what the school does already
> * new ideas for what the school could do
> * any other aspects of this topic.

1. Answer the four questions above – who, what, why and how – to work out what the task is asking you to do.

ResultsPlus Exam tip

⚠ Use the bullet points in the writing task to give you ideas for what to write about.

Once you know what you have to write about, you need to plan your ideas quickly. In the examination, spend no more than 10 minutes planning your answer. Below are two different types of plan you can use:

1 A list of points to write about

Start with the suggested bullet points from the writing task and add to them.

- **Description of local community and needs:**
  - Single mums with young kids, retired people, shops, unemployed people, high-rise flats.
  - Needs: social events and places to meet, further education/business resources
- **What the school already does:**
  - Rents out school buildings for clubs and activities
  - Holds events like fundays, fashion week, charity fundraising
- **New ideas:**
  - Use the canteen to provide cheap meals for elderly people
  - Run evening classes for adults
  - Hold conferences during the holidays

2 A spider diagram

Write the subject in the circle and draw lines from it with the bullet point suggestions at the end. Look at this example.

ACTIVITY 2

Look back at the mobile phone writing task on page 100.

1 Make two plans for the writing task:

　　a) a list of points　　　　**b)** a spider diagram.

2 Which method of planning was best at helping you work out your ideas? Use this method of planning in the examination.

ResultsPlus Exam tip

▲ Check your plan fits the writing task. Then number the points in the order in which you will write about them.

6 Planning

This lesson will help you to…

* organise your ideas into a clear and effective structure

You need to organise the ideas you generated so that you can structure your response clearly. It's important to make a good plan quickly so that you can spend your time writing.

First work out the purpose, audience and form of the writing task you have been given. Note any features your text needs to include.

Read the task below and the notes around it to see how you start your planning.

Purpose = argue so give my opinion and reasons and evidence and examples

Audience = Head Teacher

Form = Letter

- 2 addresses, date and name
- First paragraph introduces subject of letter
- Each paragraph makes a different point – use the bullets
- Final paragraph states what I want to happen as a result of my letter
- End with Yours sincerely and my signature

Write a letter for your Head Teacher arguing that your school could do more to make sure that students are prepared for real life when they leave. You may like to include:

- any practical skills that students should be taught
- information that students could be given
- opportunities that students could have
- any other aspects of this topic.

ACTIVITY 1

Look again at the writing task above.

1 Copy and complete the following sentences to explain how you should write for the audience given.

a) *The audience is … so the text should be* formal / informal.

b) *It should use correct grammar and punctuation but not … or slang.*

If you are taking the Foundation examination, you will be given bullet points that suggest what you could write about. Use these to help you make a paragraph plan.

- Jot down the ideas the points give you. You might make a spider diagram or a list (see Lesson 5). For example, the first bullet point in the task above suggests that you write about any practical skills that students should be taught. Note down your ideas on this point:

Skills students should be taught:
- *Managing money*
- *Budgeting*
- *Parenting*
- *Getting on with other people, e.g. ways of sorting out arguments*

- Use these notes to decide what the main point of each paragraph will be and what smaller points you will include in that paragraph.

- Remember to include introduction and conclusion paragraphs in your plan if they are suitable for the form you are asked to write in.

Here is an example of part of a paragraph plan for the task on page 102.

Intro: Para 1 I've spent 5 years at Rochdale Comprehensive; suggest ways to prepare pupils for life after school:

- Qualifications not always enough
- Parents not always helpful/aware

Para 2 Info to give students

- Leaver's pack of resources — benefits, Citizens Advice, library, hospitals, doctors

ACTIVITY 2

Look at the remaining three bullet points in the writing task:

- information that students could be given
- opportunities that students could have
- any other aspects of this topic.

1 Make a note of ideas that you could include in your text for each point.

2 Use your notes to complete the paragraph plan that is started above.

ACTIVITY 3

1 Write a plan for the following task. Aim to finish it in 10 minutes.

Write a speech for your local council in which you review the experience of being a teenager living in your area. You may like to include:

- what is good about living in your area
- the way teenagers are viewed and treated in the area
- any difficulties that teenagers face living in your area
- any other aspects of this topic.

7 Writing openings

This lesson will help you to…

* begin your writing clearly and effectively

The opening of your text is your chance to grab the reader's attention and impress the examiner with your writing. Some options for openings are:

- a relevant event
- a rhetorical question (one that doesn't require an answer)
- a fact
- an opinion (yours or an expert's)
- a humorous comment
- a blunt statement of your point
- a short, appropriate description.

Your audience and purpose will affect the type of opening you choose. Always ask yourself these questions:

- Would this type of opening help my text achieve its purpose?
- Would this type of opening suit my audience?

Below are four possible openings for the following task:

Write an article for your school magazine encouraging students to get fit.

A: How fit would you like to be? Fit enough to run for the bus so you can have an extra five minutes in bed every morning?

B: No one should ever be forced to get fit! Most PE teachers do a great job of putting people off exercise for life.

C: If you want to live a long healthy life then you need to get fit and stay fit.

D: To keep fit, everyone should do 30 minutes of exercise three times a week.

ACTIVITY 1

1 Look at the openings above. Identify what type of opening has been used in A, B, C and D.

A: rhetorical question

2 Would opening A, B, C or D suit the audience and purpose of the writing task best? Why?

ACTIVITY 2

1 Work out four different ways of writing the opening sentence(s) for the following writing task. Write your answers in a chart like the one below.

Write a page for your school website commenting on the events of the last year.

Types of opening	My opening sentence(s)	Ranking
Question		
Blunt statement		
Opinion		
Humour		

2 Rank your openings. Give 1 to the opening that will be most suitable for your audience and purpose and 4 to the opening that will be least suitable for them.

Practise finding ways to improve your writing openings.

- Can you make the meaning clearer?

- Are there words you can remove or change to give it more impact?

- Should you change the order of ideas or words to give them more impact?

For example:

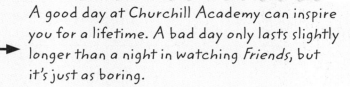

A bad day can feel like it ~~goes on and on for ever and ever~~ lasts forever and is really boring. A good day at Churchill Academy can ~~last~~ inspire you for a lifetime. ➝ A good day at Churchill Academy can inspire you for a lifetime. A bad day only lasts slightly longer than a night in watching *Friends*, but it's just as boring.

ACTIVITY 3

Below are three opening sentences that student Alissa wrote for the following writing task:

Write a review of your school for a parents' website called goodschoolguide.com.

A Churchill Academy will give your child a good education if they work hard.

B Only rats and nerds enjoy life at Churchill Academy. Sensible pupils hate the food.

C At Churchill Academy we pride ourselves on helping every student make the best of whatever talents and ability they have.

1 Which opening will suit the audience and purpose best? Why?

2 Which openings should Alissa reject?

3 How could Alissa improve her best opening? Rewrite her sentence.

8 Linking paragraphs

This lesson will help you to...

* make your writing flow from one paragraph to the next

You need to turn the ideas in your paragraph plan (see Lesson 6) into a whole text. Using **connectives** such as 'firstly', 'secondly', 'finally', 'however', and 'on the one hand…, on the other hand…' will link your paragraphs and help your writing to flow.

Below is a table showing connectives and how they can be used. Try them out as often as you can in your writing before you sit the examination.

You can link to the point you have already made by...	Connectives
adding	also, too, in addition, similarly
differing	but, however, nevertheless, although, though, on the one hand… on the other hand…, whereas, in contrast, alternatively
reinforcing	besides, anyway, after all
explaining more fully	for example, for instance, in other words, in that, that is to say
listing points in order of importance	first/firstly…, second/secondly…, finally/lastly, in the first place, first of all, to begin with, after that
showing your next point is a result of what you have just said	therefore, as a result, so, then, now that, so that
explaining	because, since, so, then, if, unless, in case, provided that, whether… or…
showing time	when, before, after, afterwards, then, since, while, meanwhile, until, till, later, as, once, whenever

Texts A and B below are two versions of the same piece of writing. They show how using connectives can make a big difference to your writing.

Text A

Our school should spend more money on making the place feel brighter and cleaner. It really makes you feel down if you spend all day in dark, messy, dirty rooms. If you are in bright, clean, well-organised rooms you feel better. It makes you feel more like working.

The school should involve students in working out the menus for school lunches. We need a better range of food that people actually like to eat. The cook gives us just what they think we should eat. A lot of food gets wasted.

Text B

Firstly, our school should spend more money on making the place feel brighter and cleaner. This is important because it really makes you feel down if you spend all day in dark, messy, dirty rooms. However, if you are in bright, clean, well-organised rooms you feel better. As a result it makes you feel more like working.

Secondly, the school should involve students in working out the menus for school lunches. This is because we need a better range of food that people actually like to eat. However, at the moment the cook gives us just what they think we should eat. As a result a lot of food gets wasted.

ACTIVITY 1

1 List the connectives used in Text B.

2 For each connective, write a sentence explaining how it links one idea to the next. Use the table of connectives to help you. For example:

'As a result' shows the next point is a result of the previous one.

ACTIVITY 2

Read Andrew's text about school leavers' parties below.

When you leave school it's really nice to have a party for the whole year group. It will be the last time they are all together. It feels really flat if there is nothing. A leavers' party is a way of celebrating all the good things you have done together before you all go your separate ways.

A leavers' party should be something that everyone can join in. I don't think it should be a really expensive event. Some schools have really fancy proms. You have to go in a suit or a posh dress and that is too much for some people. It needs to be something everyone can go to and have fun at.

1 Rewrite the text, using connectives to improve it.

The first sentence of each paragraph should introduce the main idea of that paragraph. Look again at the first paragraph of Andrew's text above. It begins with a **topic sentence** telling readers the paragraph will be about reasons for having a leavers' party.

ACTIVITY 3

Look at the whole of Andrew's text above.

1 What is the second topic sentence?

2 What does it tell readers the rest of that paragraph will be about?

Working out a paragraph plan before you begin writing (see Lesson 6) will help you to know what your topic sentences will be about. Remember: topic sentences need to tell your reader what the rest of the paragraph is about.

This is Andrew's plan for his third paragraph about school leavers' parties:

> Paragraph 3: Ways to have cheap but fun leavers' parties
> - Everyone wears 'wrecked school uniform'
> - Keeping food costs down
> - Decorations — competition between classes — prize for best area?
> - Ask businesses for donations

ACTIVITY 4

1 Use Andrew's paragraph plan to help you write a topic sentence for the third paragraph.

2 Write the rest of the paragraph using connectives to show readers how the ideas link together. The paragraph should be no more than 60 words in total.

3 Write **two** paragraphs for each of the following writing tasks. Practise using connectives and topic sentences as you write:

A: Write a speech to persuade your school or college council that every school should hold an event for the group that is leaving.

B: Write a blog entry on a website for teenagers arguing for or against the idea that 'watching sport is a waste of time'.

ResultsPlus Self assessment

Check your answer to **Activity 4**. Have you:
- used the **opening sentence** of each paragraph to help your reader understand what the paragraph will be about?
- used **connectives** to link the paragraphs together, such as 'firstly' or 'however'?
- used the **key word** from the task and words that mean the same as the key word throughout your writing to show you have stayed on topic?

Here is an example of an examination question you could be expected to answer. You will be expected to write a letter with paragraphs that link together effectively.

Write a letter to students in which you persuade them that a trip in term time EITHER would be a good idea OR would not be a good idea.

You may wish to include some of these topics to help you write your article:

- experience of travelling
- attendance at school
- safety
- friendship
- other ideas you may have.

(24 marks)

ACTIVITY 5

Write two paragraphs for the letter to students. Focus on how well you link the paragraphs together.

You should spend 10 minutes on this task.

ResultsPlus Self assessment

Before you complete this self-assessment activity you might like to read some sample answers to this task on the following pages (110 – 111).

Check your answer to Activity 5:
- Does your **opening sentence** clearly introduce what the paragraph is about?
- Do you use words such as **'however'** and **'also'** to move between paragraphs?
- Does each paragraph include a **separate topic**?

Write two paragraphs for the letter to students. Focus on how well you link the paragraphs together.

Here are three student answers to the letter task on page 109. Around and after the answers are examiner comments. Read both the student answers and examiner comments. Then complete the activity at the bottom of page 111.

Some attempt to use a topic sentence

There are some points for and some against going on holiday when you are meant to be at school but I can only really think of loads of bad points. You'd have to catch up on everything and you wouldn't get what teacher was saying in lessons so that would make it really hard to listen to what they were saying. You would get it cheaper and you would be able to use friends notes and then you can learn when you are there which is sometimes more interesting than geography were you are sat in a room for an hour.

There should be a change in paragraph here

Examiner summary

This part of the answer is typical of grade E performance. The student has tried to use topic sentences, but they suggest they are only going to look at the bad points. However, the paragraph clearly goes on to talk about good points as well as bad points. The student needed to change paragraph when it starts 'You would get it cheaper...' because they have started to talk about positive points.

Opening sentence introduces what the paragraph is about

Some may argue with me that taking time out of a term to go abroad is nothing but an upset as it takes time out of the curriculum to go and enjoy yourself well. Well they are wrong because we have tried this scheme in other schools in your area and the success rates in GCSE were a big improvement, as before they averaged at 20 – 30% but now they are achieving 60 – 75% achieving A* - C.

The advantages of travelling abroad in school time is that students get to see what travelling abroad is like. They get to know what to do at the airport and what to do when booking a hotel. Pupils get to travel round the resorts on their own and can find things.

Although on the same topic as the previous paragraph, this is a completely new idea that isn't linked to the first paragraph

Examiner summary

This part of the answer is typical of grade D performance. There is some sense that the structure is clear because the student has used a sentence at the beginning of each paragraph that links to the topic of the letter. However, there is no real connection between the two paragraphs – the only link is that both paragraphs develop an idea on a similar topic.

Having school trips in term time can have an effect on pupils because it means that they will not be attending school and this will affect their attendance. 75% of children who have low attendance in school on average do not get good results in their GCSEs than pupils who have good attendance. Mr Whitehead of OfSted said, "it is essential that children get to school as much as they can to get the best results possible."

Also, travelling to a foreign country could be bad because pupils in the class with their friends may act the clown and show off. Over the last 5 years schools trips that went abroad have had a 50% increase in violence than school trips that stayed in England.

> Opening sentence clearly focuses on the topic of the letter

> Use of a discursive marker shows this is a further idea why travelling abroad is a bad idea

Examiner summary

This part of the answer is typical of grade C performance. Student 3 has also used an opening sentence that links to the topic of the letter. This gives the writing a clear sense of structure. The use of 'Also' helps to link the paragraphs and gives the reader an understanding that the second paragraph offers another suggestion as to why school travel during term time is a bad idea.

ResultsPlus
Build better answers

Move from a Grade Ⓔ to Grade Ⓓ
In this part of your task you need to make sure you change paragraphs at the appropriate point. Student 1 has tried to use a topic sentence but then forgotten to change paragraph when they stopped exploring the bad points of holidays in term time. Student 2 changes paragraph appropriately and uses a different topic sentence for each idea.

Move from a Grade Ⓓ to Grade Ⓒ
In this part of your task you need to link paragraphs using topic sentences and discursive markers. Student 2 has linked ideas at the beginning of the paragraphs to the topic of the letter. Therefore, the response appears to be clearly structured. Student 3 used a discursive marker between paragraphs to show how one topic links to the next.

PUTTING IT INTO PRACTICE

1 Explain to a partner how to link paragraphs in a piece of writing. Use as few words as possible in your explanation.

2 Draw a diagram that will help you to remember how to link paragraphs in a piece of writing.

9 Choosing vocabulary

This lesson will help you to...

* select appropriate vocabulary that makes your writing clear and effective

Spend time in the examination making sure that the words you write are **precise**, so that your reader knows exactly what you mean, and are the best you can use to achieve your purpose.

- Choose words that explain or describe exactly what you mean. For example:

  She needs to get out there and do something about it. ✗

  To improve her game she needs to do more training. ✓

- Try to use the correct names and terms for what you are trying to say. For example:

  They should have a bit of a kick about. ✗

  They should practise their passing and dribbling skills. ✓

- Include details. For example:

  His low passes could be better. ✗

  If he used his instep and drove through the ball then his low passes would be much better. ✓

ACTIVITY 1

Look at the following writing task:

> Write a magazine review of a trip you have been to recently, like a sporting event, a concert or a visit to the cinema. Include suggestions about how the trip could be improved.

1 Write **two** paragraphs of the review. Make your vocabulary as precise as possible by:

- using words that explain or describe exactly what you mean
- using correct names and terms
- including details.

ResultsPlus Exam tip

▲ When you are thinking about what to write, list as many words that would be good to include as you can – aim for about 15 really clever words. When you are writing, try to use each word once in your response.

Try to choose powerful vocabulary that catches readers' interest and helps them to imagine what you are describing or to feel the way that you want them to. This is especially important when you are explaining or persuading.

- Powerful **verbs** can show people's opinions or feelings and grab readers' attention. For example:

'Our paper only reported what happened,' said editor Jem Murray. ✗

'Our paper only reported what happened,' argued editor Jem Murray. ✓

Bikers are often written about by the media. ✗

Bikers are often attacked by the media. ✓

- Powerful **adjectives** and **adverbs** help to describe accurately a situation or the feelings involved. For example:

Although many people think of golf as a sport best left to the middle-aged and elderly, in fact it is a game that suits everyone. ✗

Although many people think of golf as a boring sport best left to the lazy middle-aged and fragile elderly, in fact it is a challenging game that suits everyone. ✓

ACTIVITY 2

Read Siobhan's text below. She is trying to persuade people to make better use of her local swimming pool.

At the moment it is free for children under sixteen and adults over sixty to swim at our local pool. Taking your kids swimming is a trip out. It also means they'll be getting some exercise and having fun too. If your children are old enough to swim without you then it's a chance for you to do some exercise too. The main pool is kept free for people aged over sixty for an hour each day which means it is a chance for you to meet other people like you, and you know you can swim without worrying about being splashed or bumped by children.

1 Rewrite the text to make it more persuasive, changing verbs and/or adding describing words in at least **five** places.

ACTIVITY 3

1 Write a response to the following writing task using precise and powerful vocabulary that helps to achieve the task's purpose:

Write a leaflet persuading visitors and local people to make full use of the places and activities that they can enjoy in your local area.

10 Using effective punctuation and sentences

This lesson will help you to...

* select appropriate punctuation that makes your writing clear and effective

* use different kinds of sentences in your writing

Punctuation helps the reader to understand your text and its meaning. Write carefully in the examination – don't rush. This will help you to get your punctuation right.

Practise thinking about how to punctuate each sentence. Follow these steps:

First say the sentence in your head before you write it down.

Then ask yourself:

> Does that make sense? Can I say it more clearly? What punctuation do I need to use when I write it down?

Remember: sentences, names and places begin with a capital letter. Questions need a question mark at the end.

ACTIVITY 1

Look at the different punctuation marks in the box.

1 Write **seven** sentences. Use each punctuation mark at least once.

2 Write a paragraph in response to the following writing task. Focus on punctuating your sentences correctly.

> Write a website article for teenagers suggesting ways to make their money go further.

full stop **.**	comma **,**	question mark **?**
exclamation mark **!**	speech marks **' '**	
apostrophe **'**	CAPITAL LETTERS	

Remember: There are **four** different ways of writing a sentence. Here are the four **sentence types**. Aim to use a variety of sentence types when you write. Varying **sentence length** will also make your writing more interesting to read. Using a short sentence after some longer ones will make that particular point really stand out.

* A **question** – to make your readers think about your ideas.

  Should steroids be allowed in sport?

* A **statement** – to give facts or opinions.

  Steroids are used to gain weight and power.

* A **command** – to tell your reader to do something.

  Stop taking steroids.

* An **exclamation** – to express strong feelings.

  Steroids are dangerous!

ACTIVITY 2

Look at the following statement: *Homework is an important part of learning.*

1 Rewrite the statement in the form of a question, a command and an exclamation.

2 Write a paragraph in response to the following writing task. Use **at least one** example of each type of sentence.

> Write a speech for your class discussing the topic 'Television shouldn't be a part of daily life'.

Use **connectives**, or linking words, to help your reader follow the logic of your writing. See the table on page 106 for a list of the different connectives you can use.

You can also **craft** your sentences so they achieve your purpose:

- In an argument or persuasive text, rhetorical questions will push your reader to agree with your point of view.

  After all, no one wants inequality to continue, do they?

- In an argument or persuasive text, place the information you want your reader to notice most at the beginning of the sentence.

  Too many children in the west are becoming fat and unhealthy **while children starve to death in Africa.** ✗

  Children starve to death in Africa *while too many children in the west are becoming fat and unhealthy.* ✓

ACTIVITY 3

Read the text below.

Teenage boys who want to do well in sport are sometimes tempted to take steroids. They think it will give them an edge. It's true that steroids can make them gain weight and power. Steroids will also do a lot of damage. Steroids can make you vomit and pass blood, damage your liver and kidneys, give you stomach ulcers, a heart attack and change your personality so that you get angry really quickly. Famous body builders Arnold Schwarzenegger and Sergio Olivia both stopped using steroids after they found out the damage they could do to their bodies. They realised their health was more important than how fast they could grow their muscles.

1 Rewrite the text, using what you have learned in this lesson about punctuation and sentences to make it more interesting and persuasive. You may wish to:

- add connectives
- change verbs, adverbs and adjectives
- change sentence types and lengths
- reorder sentences

11 Checking and editing your writing

This lesson will help you to...

* check that your work is accurate and effective

Get into the habit of **checking** and **editing** your writing. Checking your work means looking for any mistakes in your writing and fixing them. Editing means trying to improve your writing by making better choices, such as with vocabulary and sentence structure.

Even small changes make your writing better. Make sure you are always editing and checking as you write. Ask yourself these questions:

Checking:

- Have I stayed on the subject mentioned in the brief?
- Does each of my paragraphs match the audience, purpose and form?
- Have I used a new paragraph when I have changed topic?
- Can I understand the meaning of my sentences?

Editing:

Remember: good writing is clear, varied and powerful.

- Can I make the meaning of any sentences or paragraphs clearer?
- Have I used different types and structures of sentence?
- Can I change vocabulary to add meaning?

You may have only a few minutes to check what you have written in the examination, so just check your spelling, vocabulary, punctuation and sentences for any mistakes that you can put right quickly and simply:

- **Spelling:** Is that word spelled correctly? Do I need to try again?
- **Vocabulary:** Do the words I have chosen make sense?
- **Punctuation:** Have I punctuated correctly?
- **Sentences:** Do my sentences make sense?

ACTIVITY 1

Here are a few words that are often spelled incorrectly or mixed up.

too/two/to	their/they're/there	of/off/'ve	we're/were/where	you're/your

1 Learn the correct meanings for each word.

2 Create a sentence for each group of words that uses each example. For example:

*I want **to** have **two** cars **too**.*

ResultsPlus Exam tip

▲ Check your work the whole time you're writing – not just at the end. Write a paragraph from your plan, stop, check and continue. Repeat this all the way through the exam. At the end you will then be able to check for basic things like spellings and punctuation – rather than trying to put big things right in a short amount of time.

Here is an example of an examination question. As part of your answer to it, you will be expected to check and edit your work, making the best possible choices.

> Write a letter to students in which you persuade them that a trip in term time EITHER would be a good idea OR would not be a good idea.
>
> You may wish to include some of these topics to help you write your article:
>
> - experience of travelling
> - attendance at school
> - safety
> - friendship
> - other ideas you may have.
>
> (24 marks)

ACTIVITY 2

Write a paragraph of the letter to students. Focus on how well you check and edit your work to make the best possible choices.

You should spend 10 minutes on this task.

ResultsPlus
Self assessment

Before you complete this self-assessment activity you might like to read some sample answers to this task on the following pages (118 – 119).

Check your answer to Activity 2:
- Have you checked your **spelling**?
- Have you made sure you use a **variety** of words and punctuation?
- Have you **varied the sentences** you have used and have you written these sentences accurately?

Write a paragraph of the letter to students. Focus on how well you check and edit your work to make the best possible choices.

Here are three student answers to the letter task on page 117. Around and after the answers are examiner comments. Read both the student answers and examiner comments. Then complete the activity at the bottom of page 119.

Student 1 – Extract typical of a grade Ⓔ answer

> I don't think people should be allowed to go in term time as there are too many things to get done and for the people who are in class it waistes there time to cause the teacher has to stop and explain things to them. Then you have to think about the exams that people who go on trips need to do then you can see that it is a stupid idea to do anything when you are meant to be learning the stuff that you are meant to be doing.

There are some errors in spelling, but there are also a lot of words spelled correctly

There are errors in the accuracy of sentences. There are some full stops and capital letters used

Examiner summary

This part of the answer is typical of grade E performance. This extract uses some full stops and capital letters, and there are a lot of words spelled correctly. However, the student needs to look carefully at their use of punctuation because they tend to use run-on sentences.

Student 2 – Extract typical of a grade Ⓓ answer

> Another point is that if you take a trip abroad there is a big chance that you may lose one of the pupils or one of them may run away and in a country which the language is different that could be life threatening. In the last 3 years over 1000 children aged 12 – 16 have gone missing in Spain on school trips and family holidays. Head of the directgov website Mr Baldwin said 'It is ok taking a few people on a trip but 1 full class is not good in case you lose a pupil or members of the class bully that pupil into running away.

Attempting to use a variety of sentences. However, this needs splitting into two different sentences

Accurate punctuation and apt for this piece of writing

Spelling is accurate but the vocabulary choices are quite basic

Examiner summary

This part of the answer is typical of grade D performance. Student 2 has used mostly accurate spelling and punctuation, although the choices they have made lack ambition – this means the examiner thinks it is easier for this student to be accurate than someone who has made difficult choices. Examiners much prefer ambition than accuracy! The student has attempted to use a variety of sentences, but the opening sentence is too long. The student should have used punctuation to split this up.

Repetition of the words 'pressure' and 'stress' – good word choices but more variety needed

Accurate sentences but no variety of punctuation used

> Students should take holidays in term time to get away from the stress placed on them by teachers. Many pupils feel like their teachers put too much pressure on them to complete work in deadlines which are impossible. 78 out of 89 students thought that teachers where putting too much pressure on them and that this affected their health and confidence. Sarah Cook, a pupil in an all girl school, took a two week holiday in term time to get a brake from all the stress. She felt like this helped her to reach her deadlines because she had a better approach to her work.

Some checking needed but spelling mostly accurate

Examiner summary

This part of the answer is typical of grade C performance. Student 3's response is mostly accurate but they do need to make sure that their choice of words is accurate – 'where' and 'brake' are inaccurate. The vocabulary is appropriate for a formal letter about holidays, but Student 3 could have varied the words used to describe pressure and stress a little more.

ResultsPlus
Build better answers

Move from a Grade Ⓔ to Grade Ⓓ
In this part of your task you need to make sure you are splitting up sentences accurately. Student 1 has used a number of run-on sentences, where one sentence has been linked to another with no use of punctuation. They need to practise using more full stops. Student 2 does better at organising their ideas into sentences.

Move from a Grade Ⓓ to Grade Ⓒ
In this part of your task you need to make sure your work is accurate and precise. Student 2 made a number of mistakes, whereas Student 3 ensured that they were accurate. In addition, Student 3 demonstrated that they could structure sentences well. Student 2 included a greater variety of punctuation but Student 3 achieved a grade C because the paragraph was clear and accurate.

PUTTING IT INTO PRACTICE

1 Look back over a paragraph that you have written in class. You should select a paragraph that was written under pressure. Check and edit the paragraph to ensure that it is accurate but also that it includes a variety of word, punctuation and sentence choices.

Assessment Practice: Sample Exam Paper

GCSE English Language
FOUNDATION TIER

SECTION B: WRITING

Answer **ONE** question in this section.

EITHER

*9   Your local council is planning some changes and has asked you to write a review of community facilities for young people.

Write a review which includes suggestions for future improvements.

In your review, you may wish to consider:

- a general introduction on existing community facilities for young people in your area
- any gaps in community facilities for young people
- affordable ideas for community facilities for young people
- why the new community facilities would be welcome
- any other ideas you may have.   (24)

OR

*10 Write an article for an information guide recommending a place of interest in the UK that might be enjoyable to visit.

In your article, you may wish to consider:
- features that make the place worth visiting
- any helpful hints or tips for the visit
- any other ideas you may have.   (24)

TOTAL FOR SECTION B = 24 MARKS

TOTAL FOR PAPER = 64 MARKS

GCSE English
FOUNDATION TIER

SECTION C: WRITING

Answer EITHER Question 11 OR Question 12 in this section.

EITHER

*11 Write a magazine article for parents with the title 'What makes a good school'?

You may wish to use some of these topics to help you write your article:
- behaviour and discipline codes
- teachers
- extra curricular activities
- buildings and facilities
- other ideas you may have.   (48 marks)

OR

*12 Write a speech on the topic of 'Stress and Modern Life' to be given to a group of your peers.

You may wish to include:
- what you mean by stress
- the main causes of stress in modern life
- positive suggestions on how people might cope with stress
- other ideas you may have.   (48 marks)

TOTAL FOR SECTION B = 48 MARKS

TOTAL FOR PAPER = 96 MARKS

Unit 3 Creative English: Writing

This unit is for GCSE English. If you are taking GCSE English Language, turn to page 156 for Unit 3 Spoken Language.

The Creative English unit gives you the opportunity to:

- develop your speaking and listening skills
- study a selection of poems
- produce your own piece of creative writing.

This student book unit focuses on the creative writing task and helps you to develop your creative writing skills. You will:

- read different examples of fiction writing (narratives, descriptions, monologues and scripts)
- learn how to produce your own creative writing.

Your creative writing task will be written in response to a piece of stimulus material. The stimulus material is given to you in order to spark ideas for your writing. There are lots of different stimulus materials and activities in this section of the book for you to practise with.

You will also see how professional writers create effective fiction writing. You can try to use similar techniques in your own writing.

The texts and activities you will encounter as you develop these skills are all focused on helping you to achieve the best grade you can in your Unit 3 controlled assessment task.

Your assessment

This unit is a controlled assessment unit for GCSE English. You will complete **one** creative writing task which you will have **two hours** to complete. The task will be based on one of four themes: *Relationships, Clashes and collisions, Somewhere, anywhere* or *Taking a stand*.

You will be given stimulus material based on the chosen theme (this could be an image, podcast or video clip) and asked to write a narrative, description, monologue or script in response to a task. You can write up to 1000 words in your response.

Your response to the task must show that you can:

✔ write clearly, effectively and imaginatively in a chosen form to engage your reader

✔ make sure that you spell, punctuate and use grammar accurately and appropriately for the purpose of your writing and to achieve the desired effect.

Assessment Objectives

Your Unit 3 Creative English controlled assessment response will be based on how well you:

✔ Write clearly using forms and appropriate vocabulary.

✔ Organise information and ideas.

✔ Use a range of sentence structures with accurate punctuation and spelling.

This student book unit will help you write a successful response to your controlled assessment creative writing task.

1 Generating ideas

This lesson will help you to...

* respond to an image, a video or a podcast

* develop appropriate and engaging ideas to include in your writing

You will be asked to write a piece of creative writing in response to a stimulus that you will be given, such as an image, a video or a podcast.

Look at this example of a task:

> Look at the image. Write a text which explores EITHER the events leading up to this moment OR the events which directly follow this moment.

You need to use the **stimulus** to come up with ideas that will interest your readers. You can write a **narrative**, a **description**, a **monologue** (one character's speech or thoughts spoken to themselves and the audience) or a **script**.

If the stimulus is an **image**, look at its details and ask yourself these questions:

1 What is the **first** thing you **focus** on?

2 Where do you think this is?

3 If there are **people** in the image ask yourself:

* Who is this character?

* How do they feel? Why?

* What might they want? Why?

* What might they have done?

* What could be the result of this?

* What choice might they be about to make? What effect might it have?

4 If there are **no people** in the image ask yourself:

* Who would want to visit this place? Why?

5 What **emotion** do you feel when you first look at the picture? Why?

6 What has just happened?

7 What does the image **remind** you of?

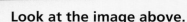

ACTIVITY 1

Look at the image above.

1 Use the questions above to produce some ideas you could use to write a piece of creative writing inspired by the image. Write down some notes as you are answering the questions.

ResultsPlus Controlled assessment tip

Write down everything that comes into your head when looking at the stimulus material – you can always cross it out later and no one will ever know! Think: **no idea is a bad idea**.

If the stimulus is a **video**, watch it several times and ask yourself these questions:

1 **Where** is this?

2 **Who** is here?

3 **Why** are they here?

4 **What** is happening?

5 **Which character** will I choose to write about?

6 Is my character an **onlooker** or **part of the action**?

7 **Why** are they here?

8 What can they **see** and **hear**?

9 What do they **experience**?

10 What are their **thoughts**? Why?

11 What are their **feelings**? Why?

ACTIVITY 2

Watch the Big Cat Diary video on the ActiveTeach several times.

1 Use the questions above to help you note down ideas you could use to write a response to the video.

If the stimulus is a **podcast**:

- Have a blank piece of paper in front of you as you listen.

- Doodle on the paper any thoughts or images that come into your mind that link to what you are hearing.

- Then write notes around your doodles. If you get stuck, use the question 'What if…?' to help you think of more ideas.

ACTIVITY 3

Listen to the podcast on underground Coventry on the ActiveTeach.

1 As you listen, doodle any images the podcast suggests to you. Below is an example of a doodle created by one student.

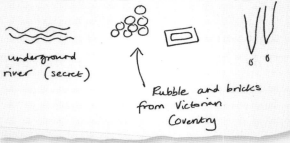

underground
river (secret)

Rubble and bricks
from Victorian
Coventry

2 Write notes and use 'What if…?' questions to help you come up with ideas for a narrative suggested by what you hear.

What if …I were underground Coventry city centre?

…I were alive during the war, or during the Victorian age?

…I spent my time exploring caves and old structures? What would I find?

Coventry's full of rubble. Because of, em, the blitz after the war much of the city centre was flattened, and the banks of the river were built up with the rubble and if you go further out of the city there's piles of rubble and that, and it's all just from war-torn Coventry when they were doing the redevelopment, which is the same time that the covert was built. So much of this stuff you're treading on is Victorian Coventry, you know, as it was.

125

2 Writing a narrative

This lesson will help you to...

* work out the plot for your story

* plan different features of your story

When you write a **narrative**, or a story, you first have to decide what it will be about. Keep your narrative simple. You can only write a maximum of 1000 words. You earn most marks for how well you tell the story, not how clever the plot is. Plan your narrative by answering the questions in the chart below.

Planning questions	Example
1 Main character – who are they? What are they like?	Joe is a teenage boy who enjoys playing football for his local youth team. He wants to go on to be a professional player.
2 What is the main character's goal?	He wants to score a goal in the league final so that he will get noticed by the talent scouts who will be watching.
3 What is the main character's problem?	His football boots have got holes in them and the coach won't let him play in the final next week if he doesn't have new boots. Joe doesn't have enough money to buy new boots.
4 How does the main character try to overcome their problem and achieve their goal?	He decides to do car washing to raise money to pay for the new boots.
5 What goes wrong?	He has almost made enough money, but as Joe is washing the last car his money is stolen by a local gang.
6 What is the ending?	Joe tells his story to the owner of the car he was washing when he was mugged. The man is a talent scout himself and he buys Joe some boots and watches him play.
7 Setting – where is the action taking place?	In a car park where Joe washes the cars.
8 Atmosphere and mood – how should your story feel to readers?	Tense when the gang arrive.

ResultsPlus Controlled assessment tip

⚠ When writing a narrative, try to stick to simple things that you have experienced. It is more important for your writing to be believable than to be about events like wars and murders and marriages. It will be easier to write about things that have happened to you because you know what they were like.

ACTIVITY 1

Read the task below.

> Look at this image. Write a narrative which explores EITHER the events leading up to this moment OR the events which directly follow this moment.

1 Copy and complete a table like the one on page 126. Jot down ideas for a narrative answering this task.

You need to make the **characters** in your story interesting. Picture them acting out the story in your head.

- What do they look like?
- How do they react?
- What do they think?
- What do they say?

ACTIVITY 2

Work on the idea for the narrative you created in Activity 1. Picture the story you are telling like a film. Focus on each of your characters and make notes about them.

1 Name the one or two characters in your story. Describe in **20 words** their looks and personality.

Joe is 16, tall and sporty, but his tracksuit and trainers are old and worn out.

2 Note how each character reacts to the main events in the story.

Joe is frightened when he sees the gang. He's very scared when they ask him for money but he tries to talk them out of taking it.

3 Note each character's thoughts and feelings when events happen.

When he sees the gang: stay calm. What am I going to do?

4 Make notes about some conversations the characters might have during the important event.

His money is for boots, needs for match, big chance

Your narrative needs a **setting** – this is where the events happen. The stimulus material may help you to decide this. You then need to describe for your reader what the setting looks and feels like.

- List the things you want your reader to picture as they read your story.

  rows of cars, quiet and isolated car park

- Include details that appeal to as many of the five senses as possible: touch, sight, smell, taste, hearing.

  smells from local takeaway, sound of main road but quiet in the car park

ACTIVITY 3

Work on the plan for the narrative you created in Activity 1.

1 Make notes on the setting(s) where your main events happen.

When you completed the table in Activity 1, you decided what **atmosphere** and mood you wanted to create in your story. Verbs, adjectives and adverbs are used to create atmosphere. When you write your narrative:

- Use **adjectives** and **adverbs** to describe what is happening.

  Joe hit the gravel **with a thump, folded** arms **first, winded.**

- Use vivid **verbs**.

  A voice **hissed** in his ear.

  His heart was **hammering** like a champion sprinter's feet.

You can also use **imagery** to create atmosphere. Look at the text below from *Truth or Dare* by Celia Rees to see how imagery is used to create the right atmosphere.

> The crater's edge crumbled away from us. We lay, staring down into a cauldron carved out of the hillside. Fields, hedges, trees had all disappeared replaced by a great pit of bare earth. I had never seen anything like it. The sides rose sheer and at the bottom great machines rested on wheels as big as houses. Cranes stood poised, their jibs swinging like compass needles. Massive concrete mixers stood like fat-bellied dinosaurs.

The word 'cauldron' makes you think of witches who are evil.

The huge size compared with the character is threatening.

This makes you think about how sharp the jibs are.

Suggests these are giant meat-eating monsters.

ACTIVITY 4

Work on the plan you created in Activity 1 on page 127.

1 Decide what atmosphere you want to create.

2 List **five** adjectives and **five** vivid verbs you can use to help build the atmosphere you have chosen.

3 Work out **three** images you can use to build the right atmosphere for your text.

4 Write a paragraph for your narrative, using the words you have chosen to give it a strong atmosphere.

Assessment Practice

Here is an example of a controlled assessment task you could be expected to answer.

You will be expected to structure your story effectively.

Look at this image.

Write a narrative titled 'The Knock'.

(24 marks)

ACTIVITY 5

Write the first two paragraphs of the narrative titled 'The Knock'. Focus on how well you structure the narrative.

You should spend 20 minutes on this task.

ResultsPlus Self assessment

Before you complete this self-assessment activity you might like to read some sample answers to this task on the following pages (130 – 131).

Check your answer to Activity 5:
• Have you **developed** your ideas throughout your writing?
• Have you **organised** your ideas well, using paragraphs and linking paragraphs effectively?

Maximise your marks

Write the first two paragraphs of the narrative titled 'The Knock'.
Focus on how well you structure your narrative.

Here are three student answers to the narrative task on page 129. Around and after the answers are examiner comments. Read both the student answers and examiner comments. Then complete the activity at the bottom of page 131.

Student 1 – Extract typical of a grade Ⓔ answer

> When I first opened the door I was surprised to see him standing there. Then when he offered to come and show me what was in his bag I said that would be good. He then walked in and I saw that he was carrying his new helmet. Then he showed me a picture of his bike and I smiled it was amazing. It was a few weeks later that I saw on the news what had happened and I remembered that night with the photo and the bike and it made it me sad.

There is a change of time. There should have been a change in paragraph

Using 'then' to link ideas is fine once or twice. It is used too many times here

Examiner summary

This part of the answer is typical of a grade E answer. The student has failed to change paragraph even though there is a change in time. There are some words chosen but the sentences are repetitive. To improve this answer the student needed to use the word 'then' less.

Student 2 – Extract typical of a grade Ⓓ answer

> Damien was riding home from work on his motorbike. He was rushing home because he could not wait to see his brand new motorbike. When Damien got home he was not very happy because his motorbike was not parked up on the drive where he expected it. He went into the house, which was warm and went into the kitchen to make some cornflakes with cold milk. Then he went into the living room and sat on his leather sofa and watched kidulthood on his plasma screen TV.
>
> Then there was a knock at the door. Damien spilt his cereal in shock. He walked to the door very cautiously. Through the glass on the door he could see a bright yellow jacket. He opened the door to see it was his friend from work with his new motorbike.

Constant use of 'then' links ideas, but it is not always appropriate to organise actions in a narrative

Good development of an idea – helping the reader to get to know Damien

Examiner summary

This part of the answer is typical of grade D performance. Student 2 does develop the description of setting, so it gives the reader a good idea about the sort of character Damien is. The description of opening the door is linked with the word 'then' throughout. Although this helps the reader to see that there are a series of actions, it can make the narrative dull. It is important to move between ideas so that they link more carefully.

Good use of vocabulary to develop the idea of mood and setting

> When Joe got home he took off his coat which was drenched with water dripping down and splashing to the floor. It was a very dark, grey rainy day so Joe switched on the lights and the fire in the living room. He slouched down on his leather sofa and turned on his new television to watch the football match.

Clever use of a short sentence to make the knock on the door seem sudden – helps move the narrative on effectively

> There was a knock at the door. Joe decreased the volume on the remote and stood up. There was another knock at the door. As he walked cautiously towards the door, Joe felt curious as he didn't know who it could be calling at this time. Joe was feeling nervous and opened the door carefully to see a tall policeman who didn't look friendly.

A repetition of the knock on the door is appropriate to give a sense of urgency

Examiner summary

This part of the answer is typical of grade C performance. The student has done well to develop the setting appropriately in the opening paragraph. The use of a short sentence to introduce the idea of someone at the door at the start of the second paragraph is clever and moves the narrative on well. Repeating the short sentence is effective and helps develop a sense of urgency. However, the student was unable to sustain this in the final sentence of the paragraph, as the repeated idea of 'cautiously,' 'carefully' and 'nervous' is not an appropriate development of an idea.

ResultsPlus
Build better answers

Move from a Grade Ⓔ to Grade Ⓓ
In this part of your task you need to think about how you can use techniques to link ideas better. Student 1 has used 'then' too many times. Student 2 still does this, but they vary sentences to add interest to the structure. Student 2 also remembers to change paragraph.

Move from a Grade Ⓓ to Grade Ⓒ
In this part of your task you need to think about how you can use techniques such as repetition to develop ideas well. Student 2 should have avoided repetition of the word 'then' as Student 3 did. Both students develop the idea of setting appropriately, but Student 3 is able to do this more effectively when the action begins. The use of the knock on the door to begin the second paragraph is a clever structural device.

PUTTING IT INTO PRACTICE

❶ Plan out the rest of the narrative in response to the title 'The Knock'.

❷ Write the third paragraph of the narrative in response to the title 'The Knock'.

3 Writing a description

You may choose to write a **description** in response to your controlled assessment creative writing task. Your description might include a scene, people, an event or any combination of these.

You need to build a powerful description.

First list the **details** you can see:

Image A

- To describe a **person**, note down details about what they look like, their interests and their personality.

  - *The woman is in a jewellery shop.*

  - *She has dark eyes and hair.*

  - *She is wearing red earrings and a hair wrap.*

  - *She looks artistic and creative.*

  - *She looks like she likes art and jewellery and is kind and quiet.*

Image B

- To describe a **scene**, note down details about buildings, cars, people, trees.

  - *It is a busy market street with people walking up a steep hill.*

  - *There are lots of clothes and hats in the shops.*

  - *Above the shops are tall apartment buildings.*

Image C

- To describe an **event**, note down details about where it is taking place and what is happening.

  - *There is a big crowd of people watching a fireworks display on Bonfire Night.*

  - *They are in an open area, and it's late in the evening.*

Next, to make your description more effective, include things that your **senses** would experience in the place shown in the stimulus: for example, Image C might have these:

- **Sight**: *bright flames*
- **Smell**: *smell from fireworks*
- **Sound**: *dogs barking*
- **Taste**: *smoke from the fire*
- **Touch**: *hot air from the fire, cool breeze*

ACTIVITY 1

Study the photograph of the scene in Image B.

1 Make a list of **five** features of the **place** where it is happening.

2 List **five** features of **what** is happening.

3 Try to find at least **one** detail that appeals to each of the five senses.

Then choose **adjectives** to describe the details in your lists. Decide what impression you want your description to give and spend time working out which words or images will create this. For example, to give an unpleasant impression you might choose 'ugly' concrete buildings, a 'sour' breeze, 'dirty brown' leaves.

ACTIVITY 2

Look at the image.

1 Note down **five** details you would describe about these these people and their surroundings. Try to include examples of sight, sound and touch.

2 Choose the impression you should like to give in your description of this image, for example, 'sympathetic', 'negative' or 'worried'.

3 Select adjectives for your details that support the impression you want to give.

3 Writing a description

Your description will be more powerful if you can create effective images to describe details more vividly. Use **comparisons** in your description to give your reader a clear idea of what you are describing: for example, comparing a car's headlights to the eyes of a monster.

- **Similes** make a comparison using the words 'as' or 'like'.

  *The trees on the horizon **were** **like** a row of elephants walking through the desert.*

- **Metaphors** say that something is or has become the thing it is being compared to.

  *On the horizon, the trees **were** a row of elephants walking through the desert.*

When you write your description, use the **past tense** all the way through. Write as if the scene was visited a while ago.

The houses <u>were</u> all perfect.

ACTIVITY 3

One student, Amrita, has started to fill in the following table to build a set of images to describe how trees look.

1 Make a table like the one below to build **four** images to describe this scene.

Object	Compared to	Simile or metaphor
1 Tree branches	Arms waving at a concert	In the breeze, the branches swayed like fans' arms at a concert.
2		

When you are writing a description you need to choose a logical way to **organise** the information.

If you are describing a scene then give your reader an overview of the whole picture before focusing on the small details.

In the extract from *Bloodtide* on page 135, Melvin Burgess describes the territory run by a gang leader called Conor. He begins with the headquarters, describing first its boundaries and then what lies beyond them.

Conor's headquarters in Finchley occupied several whole streets, an old estate of luxury houses. It was flanked on one side by an old railway cutting, on another by a reservoir. The old North Circular road on the other side was planted with razor wire and mines and was overlooked by wooden watch towers and armed guards. A great brick wall ran right around it all. Headquarters looked like a prison from outside, but the wall was to keep the prisoners out, not in.

Burgess uses more descriptive techniques in the next two paragraphs of *Bloodtide*:

- A **strong contrast** is made between the two places being described: inside and outside the Estate.

- **Vivid verbs** give more depth to the description.

Vivid verbs

Strong contrast

All around it brickwork crumbled, doors peeled and rotted, paving stones cracked, telegraph and lamp-posts leaned, toppled and fell. Conor had a smaller population than Val but he was a hard ruler. With every second penny they earned going to Conor – it used to be called protection money but the ganglords called it tax these days – the people had little to spare.

But inside the Estate the houses were all perfect, the paintwork bright, the roads and pavements manicured to perfection. Conor took a pride in making his own place exactly as it had been in the olden times, when there was still society.

ACTIVITY 4

Look back at the image you explored in Activity 2 on page 133.

1. How would you organise your description of this scene to create a powerful description?

2. Write a paragraph of **50 words** describing the place.

3. Write a second paragraph that describes the contrast between the people and their surroundings.

4. Try to include one example of imagery in your description of the surroundings.

ResultsPlus Self assessment

Check your answer to **Activity 4**. Have you:
- used the **senses** to help build a clear picture in the readers' mind?
- linked your ideas to **familiar things** so that it is easier for your reader to see what you see?
- chosen the most **powerful adjectives** to capture the image?

4 Writing a script

This lesson will help you to...

* write in the form of a script

* reveal character and plot through what people say

You could choose to write a **script** for your controlled assessment creative writing task. More information on writing a script can be found on pages 168–171. The characters in your script must react to each other and to the events that happen. You need to work out how they will behave by deciding what your characters are like.

First answer these questions about each character:

What is the character's name?	Ethan
What kind of personality does the character have?	Ethan is laid back most of the time, but sometimes he suddenly snaps and gets really angry.
What does she/he want or need?	He wants a job because he needs the money to pay a man back. The man is getting nasty and wants his money now.
What is his/her background?	He lives on a council estate in a rough part of town.
How does he/she speak?	When he is trying to impress someone he tries to use lots of long words and speak in very polite standard English, but he doesn't always get it right.

Your script will be more interesting if your characters are quite different from one another.

ACTIVITY 1

Look at the photograph. Imagine that this is Mark, a character who will appear in a script with Ethan.

1 Work out what Mark is like by creating a table like the one above, answering the questions for him. Be sure to make him very different from Ethan.

Next work out what situation your characters are facing: for example, both being interviewed for the same job as a lifeguard.

Then work out how each character will react to the situation and what will happen. For example:

Ethan is trying to impress the boss by being very polite, so he tries to sound posh and speaks very carefully. Mark will do something that makes Ethan speak and behave in his normal manner. The surprise ending is that the boss gives Ethan the job anyway.

ACTIVITY 2

1 Imagine how Mark could try to make sure that Ethan doesn't get the job. Write down a few sentences that summarise your ideas.

2 How would Ethan react to what Mark does? Write a few sentences explaining Ethan's reaction.

Below is an example of a scene where we meet Ethan. Look at this scene to see how to format a script.

Set the scene. Give instructions about what the audience should see: how the set looks and what costumes the characters are wearing.

Stage directions telling characters how to act are placed in brackets.

Ethan is in a small office overlooking the swimming pool. He is dressed in smart casual clothes and his hair is unusually tidy. He is clearly nervous.

Ethan: I would be very reliable, hard-working, conscientious and... um, I'd always turn up on time.

Boss: (smiling) That's good to hear.

Speech is written in sentences using sentence punctuation.

Write characters' names on the left in the margin.

ACTIVITY 3

1 Write a short scene in which Mark and Ethan meet for the first time. Make sure you set your script out correctly and include the setting, speech and stage directions. You could use the script below as a start to your scene.

As the boss is taking Ethan out to walk around the pool, they run into Mark, who is about to knock on the boss's door.

Mark: Oh, hello, sir.

Boss: Hello, Mark. You're early. I was about to show Ethan around the pool. Why don't you join us? (turning to Ethan) Ethan, this is Mark. He's also interviewing to be a lifeguard here.

The way a character speaks shows the audience how they are thinking and feeling. It can also reveal things about their personality or background. A character might change the way they speak to suit different situations they are in. For example, when Mark annoys Ethan, he might react like this:

Ethan: Listen bruv' if you don't back off I'm gonna....

ACTIVITY 4

1 What is different about the way Ethan speaks to the boss and the way he speaks to Mark in the line above?

2 Why does he speak differently in these two situations?

3 How might Mark speak to the boss? Write four lines of dialogue between Mark and the boss.

4 How might Mark speak to Ethan? Think about whether this would be different from the way he speaks to the boss. Write four lines of dialogue between Mark and Ethan.

5 How might the boss speak to his wife when he tells her about the interview? Write the scene in which he arrives home and tells her about his day.

5 Writing a monologue

A **monologue** is a script where one character talks directly to the audience. The character tells you their thoughts and feelings and their reactions to what other people have said or done.

Below is an extract of a monologue from Alan Bennett's *A Cream Cracker under the Settee*.

When people were clean and the streets were clean and it was all clean and you could walk down the street and folks smiled and passed the time of day, I'd leave the door on the latch and go on to the end for some toffee, and when I came back Dad was home and the cloth was on and the plates out and we'd have our tea. Then we'd eat the toffees and listen to the wireless all them years ago when we were first married and I was having the baby.

Doris and Wilfred. They don't get called Doris now. They don't get called Wilfred. Museum, names like that. That's what they're called in Stafford House. Alice and Doris, Mabel and Gladys. Antiques. Keep them under lock and key. 'What's your name? Doris? Right. Pack your case. You belong in Stafford House.'

A home. Not me. No fear.

....

She closes her eyes. A pause.

You need to keep the story your character tells quite simple. The storyline of the whole of Alan Bennett's *A Cream Cracker under the Settee* can be summed up in three sentences:

> The old lady is living on her own and doesn't want to go into a home. When she has a fall she doesn't let anyone know because she is so scared of being made to go into a home. She lies on the floor for a long time instead.

ResultsPlus Watch out!

■ When writing a monologue, be careful that you remember who is speaking. It is easy to slip into telling a story using a narrator and forget that you are meant to be writing something for a character to speak.

ACTIVITY 1

Read the following task:

> Look at the image. Write a monologue which explores the events that lead up to this moment.

1 Answer the following questions to generate some ideas about the character that you can use in your monologue:

a) Who might your character think about, and why?

She might think about her friend because...

b) Where is your character?

c) What might have happened to your character?

d) What might your character worry about?

e) What might your character feel excited or happy about?

2 Write a **three-sentence** storyline to sum up your character's story.

A monologue is always written in the **first person** (using 'I', 'me' and so on), so your character needs to have their own voice. To work out how they will speak, see if there are any clues in the picture, like their age or the way they dress, and then decide:

- **who** your character is:

  He is a GCSE student. He likes listening to music, playing football, and going to the cinema with his mates.

- **where** they live:

  He lives in a terraced house in Liverpool with his parents and little brother.

- **how old** they are:

  He is 15.

ACTIVITY 2

Look at the creative writing task in Activity 1.

1 Read the tips above and think about how your character might speak. Try speaking in their voice. Talk about people and events in your storyline and the thoughts and worries your character might have. Make notes on what works well for your character.

2 Write your monologue in response to the task.

6 Creating characters

This lesson will help you to…

* create interesting characters

* use different techniques to show what characters are like

You may need to create characters for your creative writing task:

* In a **narrative** your characters make the action happen.

* In a **monologue** you write a speech given by a character, talking about their thoughts and feelings about events that have happened.

Good writers do not **tell** readers what characters are like. Instead, they **show** readers what a character is like through things like **appearance**, **behaviour** and **speech**. This lets the reader enjoy working out what kind of person the character is.

Read the text below to find out how this works.

Appearance – the narrator is wearing her school uniform. She doesn't normally wear this, but she is starting at a new school today.

Speech – the narrator's speech is formal. She seems more mature than her friend, Danielle, who speaks in slang and doesn't respect the new school's rules.

'Whoa!' she called out. 'Who you tryin' to impress?'

I smiled and walked over to her. 'Morning lovey,' I said, giving her a quick hug. 'How you doing?'

'Nah seriously,' she said, pulling my tie. 'What's all this?'

'Come on, Danielle. You know I'm starting at Marchmont today.'

'Oh yeah. You're bailin' on us for those poshies,' she sneered, twisting some of her pink hair around her finger.

'Let me be, ok? They're very particular about their dress code, and I don't want to get in trouble on my first day.'

'What kind of stupid school is gonna give you a hard time because I'm touching your shiny new blazer?' Danielle asked, pulling my badge until I grab her hands.

Behaviour – the narrator doesn't let Danielle mess around with her uniform. She wants to make a good impression on her first day. The writer shows the narrator can stand up to Danielle.

ACTIVITY 1

Look at the task you have been set for your creative writing controlled assessment.

1 Think about a character that you might include in your response.

2 The table below is based on the text you've just read. Use a table like this to note your ideas about:

a) what the character is like

b) how you can show this to your readers.

What the character is like	Danielle: A teenager who doesn't follow the normal rules or do what is expected. She is loud and doesn't care what people say about her.
I can show this through:	
Appearance	Mis-matched trainers, pink hair
Behaviour	Shouts at her friend, pulls at her tie and blazer
Speech	Uses teenage slang, calls her friend's new school 'the poshies'

Writers can show more about a character by writing about their **thoughts**, **feelings** and **attitudes**. Read the following text. It shows the narrator's thoughts and opinions.

> **Feelings** – the narrator likes Danielle, but she's a bit worried about her messing up her first day at a new school.

> **Attitudes** – the narrator can see why some people just see Danielle's behaviour and find her annoying, but she sees her as a true friend.

> **Thoughts** – the narrator thinks Danielle is a good friend even though she has some less pleasant qualities.

I anxiously looked for the bus. Don't get me wrong; generally I like seeing Danielle. She is one of those girls who can make me smile and forget about what's on my mind. I know some people think she's irritating, but I still cringe every time I hear someone call her 'The Storm'. She *is* loud, and she doesn't tend to pay much attention to the generally accepted rules – she doesn't wait in line to get her latte at Costa, wear matching trainers or keep quite at the cinema, and it's quite common for her to talk so loud that everyone in the restaurant can hear all about your embarrassing date last night. But if you just get to know her a little bit, you'll find a friend who will stick by your side no matter what kind of mess you find yourself in.

ACTIVITY 2

1. Add three more rows to the table you made in Activity 1. Note how you can show what your character is like through their **thoughts**, **feelings** and **attitudes**.

ACTIVITY 3

Read the two texts again.

1. Write a paragraph about the first time that the narrator and Danielle meet. Use the ideas in the chart on page 140 to help you show what the characters are like.

2. Read through your paragraph while thinking '**SHOW don't TELL**'. Find any places where you could show your readers rather than telling your readers. Make these changes.

ResultsPlus Controlled assessment tip

It is a good idea to use people you know when you are trying to build a character. You might use a number of people you know to create one character. By using people you know and giving them different names, you can make better choices about how they might look or how they might react in your writing.

7 Writing from different perspectives

This lesson will help you to...

* write from different perspectives
* create different voices

You can either write in the **first person** (e.g. 'I ran across the road') or **third person** (e.g. 'She ran across the road'). The form you choose to write in will help you decide whether to use first or third person. For example:

* A **monologue** <u>must</u> be written in the **first person** (see Lesson 5).
* A **description** is usually written in the **third person** (see Lesson 3).
* A **narrative** can be written in the **first person** ('I ran') or the **third person** ('she/he ran').

First person (**I** ran, **We** talked, This is **mine**)	Third person (**He** ran, **They** talked, This is **hers**)
The reader: • knows what the narrator thinks and feels • sees everything through the narrator's eyes and voice • learns about characters and events when the narrator does.	The reader: • can follow different characters – readers get lots of perspectives • knows thoughts and feelings of lots of characters. The writer: • can give opinions that aren't a character's opinions • can explain when characters don't understand.
For example read this extract from *Malarkey,* by Keith Gray: He scrambled over the windowsill. I wondered how long he'd been out there, because his clothes were damp and when he ran a hand over his shorn hair, the rain that had been trapped in the stubble ran down the back of his neck.	For example, read this student extract: Leo squinted up at the window. Good it was open. He should be able to climb up there if he could pull himself up on the drainpipe. Above him Mr Symes was shutting down his laptop. A cool breeze fluttered a letter moving it off the neat pile. He glanced at the window. He didn't want to come back and find his papers blown onto the floor. Better close it.

ACTIVITY 1

1 Read the explanation of first person writing above. How does the first example show that the writing is in first person?

You can read the narrator's thoughts ('I wondered how long he'd been out there') but you don't know ...

2 Read the explanation of third person writing above. How does the example show that the writing is in third person?

Different characters in the same story will have different thoughts and feelings about events.

You need to decide:

* **who** is telling your story (the **narrator**)
* **how** you are going to express their experience (the **perspective**).

ACTIVITY 2

Read the task below.

> Look at this image. Write a narrative from the viewpoint of one of the people in this image.

1 Pick **two** characters from the image. Decide:

　a) what each character is like

　b) how they each speak, think and feel

　c) what part each played in the events

　d) what dialogue went on before during and after the fight.

2 Imagine your two characters now have to tell the police how they think the fight started. Write a short paragraph in the first person from each character's perspective. You could start like this:

I was just passing the fish 'n' chips shop, like, when this bloke shouted, 'You owe me, Duffy.'

3 Now choose another person from the scene. Write a short paragraph using the third person telling how they experienced the fight. For example:

The teenager was walking along the High Street when a man shouted at him, 'You owe me, Duffy.'

ACTIVITY 3

Read the task above again.

1 Make these decisions:

　a) From which character's perspective are you going to write your narrative?

　b) How does your character speak, think and feel?

2 a) Write the first paragraph of your story from your character's viewpoint, using the first person and the words and voice your character would use.

　b) Write the first paragraph of your story again, but this time use the third person. Remember to include information about more than one character's thoughts and feelings.

3 Compare the techniques you have used to tell the story. Does first person or third person make it more engaging for your reader? Finish writing your narrative in that way.

8 Choosing the best vocabulary

This lesson will help you to...

* choose the best words to express ideas
* use vivid and varied vocabulary

Help your readers to picture what you are writing about by choosing **precise** and **interesting** words.

Being precise means choosing the best words to help your readers know exactly what something or someone is like: for example, 'child' is a general word – it includes teenagers, toddlers, babies, boys, girls and so on. 'Baby' is a more precise word.

The following extract includes some precise language.

More precise than 'teenager' or 'young', but more general than giving her exact age

> She was in her late teens, but all the boys were in love with her. She wore designer jeans and H&M Jimmy Choos. Her jet black hair, cropped fashionably at the chin, bounced as she strutted down the corridor.

More precise than 'jeans'

More precise than 'short'

ACTIVITY 1

Read this extract.

> A young girl, who looked about eighteen, was walking down the street. She was wearing blue jeans with a yellow vest top and flip flops with little yellow daisies on them.

1 Where would you place each of these descriptions on the scale below?

a) young girl   **c)** blue jeans

b) eighteen   **d)** flip flops with little yellow daisies

GENERAL ◖━━━━━━━━━━━━●━━━━━━━━━━━━◗ PRECISE

Some of the most precise descriptions in the extract include one or more **adjectives** – words that describe nouns. For example:

yellow vest top ←———————— Adjective

ACTIVITY 2

1 Rewrite the extract from Activity 1, adding or changing adjectives to make the description more precise.

ResultsPlus Watch out!

■ It is easy to repeat the same words over and over. For instance, it is easy to keep using the word 'then' at the beginning of a sentence. Your examiner is more interested in the way you write than the plot you write. Make sure you check that you have **control in the choice of vocabulary**.

You can also improve your writing by making your **verbs** more precise. Look at these three sentences:

- He **put on** his trousers and **left** the house.

- He **tugged** on his trousers and **slipped out** of the house. *This sentence uses very precise **verbs** to tell the reader how each action happened.*

- He **swiftly** put on his trousers and **silently** left the house. *This sentence uses **adverbs** to explain the action.*

ACTIVITY 3

The sentences below are very vague. The words in brackets explain what information is missing in the sentence. Rewrite the sentences as instructed to make them more precise. Your sentences should not need the words in brackets.

1 Make these sentences more precise by changing the **verbs**:

a) The man walked down the street. (slowly)

The man ambled down the street.

b) The woman talked to her friend. (casually)

2 Make these sentences more precise by adding **adverbs**.

a) He spoke to the girl (but wasn't very friendly).

b) She laughed at his joke (but didn't really find it funny).

Avoid repeating words in your writing. Try to find alternatives that mean the same thing – these are called **synonyms**.

ACTIVITY 4

Read the description below of this image.

The girl is getting married and she looks happy. Everyone around them looks happy. Her clothes are pretty. She is holding her arm up. Other people have put their hands on her head. There are flowers all around her.

1 Rewrite the paragraph, including:

a) precise nouns and verbs

b) adjectives and adverbs

c) synonyms to replace repeated words.

9 Crafting sentences

There are several different **types of sentence** you can use. In creative writing the type of sentence you choose can:

- build tension

- increase the pace of action

- surprise readers

- grab their attention.

Look at the way Marjorie Blackman uses different types of sentence to change pace and build tension in this extract from *Double Cross*.

> The long sentence slows the pace down.

> Two short sentences speed up the pace – especially after the long one. They also build tension, especially at the end of a paragraph.

> There I stood at the edge of the park, two unaddressed envelopes in my jacket pockets, an unaddressed parcel in my hands and the distinct feeling that I was being followed. The prickling of my nape left me in no doubt about that. I looked around nervously.
>
> The question was, who was watching me?

> The question sets readers thinking. As it is a short, single-sentence paragraph, it builds the pace and tension even more.

ACTIVITY 1

Read the paragraph below.

We were running through the estate, down the long paths then suddenly turning right and hurtling off in another direction. We jumped over low walls, through gardens then leapt back up over and onto another path. All the time we ran we could hear them following us and they were never far behind so we had to keep on going even though we were sweating and our hearts were banging inside us.

1 Rewrite this paragraph using different types of sentence to build tension in the writing.

2 Write the next paragraph of the story.

   a) Use long sentences to describe the situation.

   b) Follow the long sentences with a few short sentences to build tension.

   c) You may also wish to use a question.

You can also tell readers what information is important by the **sentence order**.

You can make readers notice information by placing it at the beginning of sentences. The focus in these two sentences is on the girl and how the situation is making her feel:

There I stood at the edge of the park, two unaddressed envelopes in my jacket pockets, an unaddressed parcel in my hands and the distinct feeling that I was being followed. The prickling of my nape left me in no doubt about that.

Sometimes leaving important information until the end of a sentence, especially if it is the end of a paragraph, gives it more impact:

> The question was, who was watching me?

Before you write a sentence try out different ways of writing it. Make sure readers are given the most important information when it will have most impact.

ACTIVITY 2

1 Rewrite each of the following sentences so that the reader focuses more on what the character is experiencing than on what is happening.

a) Traffic sped by, shoppers popped into stores, and children nagged for ice creams while the sweat poured down Nicola's face as she steadily washed car after car after car.

b) The biggest youth sneered and kicked away the car wash bucket and sponges as Nicola's heart pounded.

c) Taking the gang by surprise Nicola, who had stood up slowly and carefully as if stiff from crouching, suddenly sprinted off and pushed the shortest gang member to the ground.

d) As the gang gave chase, Nicola heard them shout 'Get her!' and pounding feet raging towards her.

2 Look at the sentences you have just written. Add more tension to your writing by changing some of the sentences into shorter ones, or questions.

ResultsPlus Self assessment

Check your answer to **Activity 2**. Have you:
- chosen words on purpose?
- made sure that you have chosen different **types of sentence** to keep readers interested?
- used lots of **different punctuation** so your writing has lots of different emotions in it?

10 Using paragraphs

This lesson will help you to...

* show the reader what is new in each paragraph

You must use paragraphs in your creative writing. **Paragraphs** help your reader understand your writing better because a new paragraph signals that you are going to tell them about a different **time**, **place**, **person** or **part of an event**, or a **different speaker** is going to say something.

Look at the three paragraphs below from *Fearless* by T. E. Berry. The writer begins the first sentence of each paragraph by signalling to readers what new information they are being shown.

Speech	→	'Run!' screamed Usha. 'The soldiers are here!'
New and different event	→	But the next second, a uniformed arm seized her from behind and she was dragged from the ledge. The rest of the Citizen-patrol had arrived.
Different place	→	Down on the plain, Keira took in the situation in an instant.

Begin new paragraphs with a word that can help your reader understand the flow of your ideas. The list below shows some examples of when it is appropriate to start new paragraphs with connectives (linking words).

Reasons for changing paragraph	Connectives
Time	when, before, after, afterwards, then, since, while, meanwhile, until, till, later, as, once, whenever
A new but similar idea or event	another, in the same way, also, too, in addition
A new and contrasting idea or event	but, however, nevertheless, although, though, on the one hand … on the other hand, whereas
A new idea listed in order of importance	first/firstly, second/secondly, finally/lastly, first of all, to begin with, next, after that
Place	up, down, under, on top, inside, outside, over, here

ACTIVITY 1

Read the task below.

> Look at this image. Write a text which explores EITHER the events leading up to this moment OR the events which directly follow this moment.

1 Write three paragraphs of a response to this task. Make sure that you begin each paragraph with a sentence that lets your reader know whether they are being shown a new idea, event, time, place or speech. Use the connectives in the chart above to help you.

Here is an example of a controlled assessment task you could be expected to answer.

You will be expected to craft the language you use effectively.

> Look at this image.
> Write a narrative titled 'The Knock'.
>
> (24 marks)

ACTIVITY 2

Write the final paragraph of the narrative titled 'The Knock'. You should focus on how well you craft the language that you use, including crafting sentences, choosing vocabulary, person and paragraphs.

You should spend 20 minutes on this task.

ResultsPlus Self assessment

Before you complete this self-assessment activity you might like to read some sample answers to this task on the following pages (150 – 151).

Check your answer to Activity 2:
- Have you expressed ideas **effectively**?
- Have you selected vocabulary for effect?
- Have you chosen **suitable** punctuation and sentence structures to create an effect?

Maximise your marks

Write the final paragraph of the narrative titled 'The Knock'. You should focus on how well you craft the language that you use, including crafting sentences, choosing vocabulary, person and paragraphs.

Here are three student answers to the narrative task on page 149. Around and after the answers are examiner comments. Read both the student answers and examiner comments. Then complete the activity at the bottom of page 151.

Student 1 – Extract typical of a grade (E) answer

A good first sentence, but this quality of writing isn't continued throughout the paragraph

> The knock was really loud. I walked to the door and opened the door slowly as I was worried that there was something bad on the other side of the door. There was a policeman stood there with my friend who looked red in the face and a little bit drunk as he had been out in town with other people who had left him behind. Then the policeman asked if I would look after my friend until he was not drunk anymore because he would have to take him to the police station if I didn't so I said that I would.

There are a lot of words used here when just a few would have been more powerful

Examiner summary

This part of the answer is typical of a grade E performance. The student has written a good first sentence. It is abrupt, like the knock on the door. However, the sentences become quite basic, and the student forgets to use language effectively. The words that the student chose needed more thought out – they have sometimes written lots because they haven't thought about the correct word to use.

Student 2 – Extract typical of a grade (D) answer

Good choice of vocabulary

> His father told him how the accident happened, it sounded horrendous. He was driving on the motorway, trying to see how fast the motorbike was, when his life flashed before his eyes. The next time he knew of he was waking up in the hospital. He found out he had a broken leg and a broken collar bone.

This commonly used phrase, known as a cliché, weakens the language used

Examiner summary

This part of the answer is typical of grade D performance. The sentences are clearly structured and some good word choices are made. However, there is no real evidence that the choices of words, punctuation or sentences have been used for effect. The final paragraph clearly just tells the reader what happens.

An effective short sentence to give an effect of urgency

The police arrived. Joe and the two policemen rushed upstairs to his parent's bedroom. Nobody was there. The window was wide open and a light breeze coming through. Joe was terrified, as he knew the robber had taken his mother's jewellery and escaped without being seen. A policeman took all the notes he could and he promised they would work hard to catch the man but both Joe and the policeman knew it was likely never going to be solved.

Good choice of vocabulary – makes the room seem still

Examiner summary

This part of the answer is typical of grade C performance. Student 3 has used an effective opening sentence to give a sense of urgency and the word choice 'light breeze' helps give a sense that the room is empty. This means that some choices have been made to have an effect on the reader.

ResultsPlus
Build better answers

Move from a Grade E to Grade D
In this part of your task you need to make sure that you use language accurately. Student 1 begins well with a good sentence for effect but then forgets to split up the remaining text into sentences. Student 2 does this much more accurately and also chooses vocabulary a little more precisely.

Move from a Grade D to Grade C
In this part of your task you need to start considering how you want the reader to react. Although written clearly, Student 2 has made no choices that are intended to have an effect on the reader. Instead, the student has written accurately about what happened. Student 3 improves on this by starting to make choices, particularly with sentences and some vocabulary, to impact on the reader.

PUTTING IT INTO PRACTICE

1 Write the final paragraph for a narrative titled 'A Box'. Try to include a question, a short sentence for effect and verbs that have a powerful impact on the reader.

2 Write a second final paragraph for the same narrative. Use the same techniques but try to achieve a different effect.

Controlled Assessment Practice

Guidance for students: Creative Writing Task

What do I have to do?
You will complete one task on creative writing, from a choice of four.
You must complete this task on your own.

How much time do I have?
Following preparation, you will have up to two hours to complete this task.

How do I prepare for the task?
Choose the task.

Review the stimulus material provided for the task with your teacher.
Stimulus materials will be based on themes which are shared with the
Edexcel Poetry Anthology themes; **however,** it is not necessary to study the
poems for the writing task. Any theme may be chosen.

You will be given guidance about creative writing, which may include:
- the content – real or imagined events
- your audience
- the 'voice' you may want to use
- any plot or narrative structure
- the structural features of your writing
- creation of character and use of dialogue
- creation of setting and atmosphere
- appropriate language techniques
- use of imagery
- use of rhetorical devices.

You should then prepare by making notes and planning your response to
the task.

What must my response to the task show?
The response must show that you can:
- write clearly, effectively, and imaginatively in your chosen form to
  engage the reader
- make sure your spelling, punctuation and grammatical structures are
  accurate and appropriate for purpose and effect.

How should I present my response?
A written response of up to 1000 words.

Examiner's tip

Prepare before your assessment
as much as you like, but all
writing must be completed
in the supervised controlled
assessment.

Examiner's tip

Practise making your writing
engaging while you prepare for
the controlled assessment.

Examiner's tip

Remember to check over your
writing before you submit it.

The Creative Writing Task for the student

Choose one theme and complete the task from the choice below.

The text may be one of the following:
- Narrative
- Description
- Monologue
- Script

Examiner's tip

Answer one task below using one of these forms.

Theme A: Relationships
Task: Look at the image.
Write a text which explores EITHER the events leading up to this moment OR the events which directly follow this moment.

(24)

Turn to page 154 to see the controlled assessment stimulus material or visit www.edexcel.com.

Theme B: Clashes and Collisions
Task: Look at the video clip.
Write a text from the viewpoint of a person in this video clip.

(24)

Theme C: Somewhere, Anywhere
Task: Look at the image.
Write a text titled 'A place of my own'.

(24)

Theme D: Taking a Stand
Task: Listen to the podcast on the website.
Write a text based on the activities of a campaigner.

(24)

Here are the stimuli for the tasks on page 153.

Relationships (image)

Robert Doisneau,
Le Baiser de l'Hotel de Ville
(1950)

Clashes and collisions (video)

Euronews
G20 London Protests

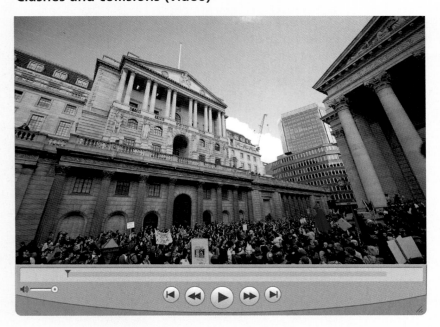

Somehere, anywhere (image)

'For Sale House Sign'

Taking a stand (podcast)

Guardian Podcast —
Paul Watson
(3 min 59)

Japan's whaling fleets in the Antarctic halted its operations today while they decide what to do with two anti-whaling activists who've been detained by the crew of a Japanese harpoon ship that they climbed on board. This is the moment it happened…

Unit 3 Spoken Language

This unit is for GCSE English Language. If you are taking GCSE English, turn to page 122 for Unit 3 Creative English: Writing.

The Spoken Language unit lets you:

- develop your speaking and listening skills
- complete a spoken language study
- write for the spoken voice.

This student book unit focuses on the spoken language study and spoken voice tasks.

In this unit you will explore both scripted speech (like TV scripts) and spontaneous speech (like your own everyday language). This section of the book will help you to:

- identify features of spoken language, both scripted and spontaneous
- understand the effects that language has on different audiences
- investigate why people use language differently in certain situations.

The texts and activities you will encounter as you develop these skills are all focused on helping you to achieve the best grade you can in your spoken language controlled assessment.

Your assessment

This unit is a controlled assessment unit for GCSE English Language. You will complete **two** writing tasks: a Spoken Language Study and Writing for the Spoken Voice.

In the **Spoken Language Study** section, you will complete **one** task from a choice of **two** in which you will be asked to explore the way spoken language works. You will have up to **two hours** to complete this task and you can write up to 1000 words. You will be given the task in advance so that you have time to plan your response.

In your response to the Spoken Language Study task, you will need to:

✔ show how spoken language changes depending on the context
✔ Understand some of the choices people make when they are speaking.

In the **Writing for the Spoken Voice** section, you will complete **one** task from a choice of **three** and write either a speech, a story with lots of direct speech, or a script for a specific media type, such as a radio drama or TV soap. You will be given either a word limit of 1000 words or a limit of the equivalent of between 30 seconds and 2 minutes of spoken language. You will be given the task in advance so that you have time to plan your response.

Your response to the Writing for the Spoken Voice task must show that you:

✔ understand that different media work in different ways
✔ understand the needs of different audiences and purposes.

Assessment Objectives

Your Unit 3 Spoken Language controlled assessment writing tasks will be based on how well you do the following:

Spoken Language Study Task

✔ Explain why language changes in different contexts.

✔ Evaluate the impact of spoken language choices.

Writing for the Spoken Voice Task

✔ Write clearly, using forms and appropriate vocabulary.

✔ Organise information and ideas.

This student book unit will help you to write a successful response to your controlled assessment writing tasks.

1 Identifying the features of spoken language

This lesson will help you to...

* understand how spoken language works

* identify some of the features of spoken language

* understand how spoken language changes depending on the situation

Spoken language is all around us every day: we talk and listen to friends, neighbours and people in shops. We also listen to spoken language on television and the radio.

ACTIVITY 1

1 Make a list of five times you have used spoken language today.

on my way to school

2 Answer the following questions for each example you listed above.

a) Where did you use it?

on the bus

b) Who were you speaking to?

the bus driver

c) Why did you use it?

to buy a ticket

There are two forms of spoken language:

* **scripted** speech, or planned speech, like you hear in films or in a formal speech

* **spontaneous** speech, or unplanned speech, like you use in conversations or answering questions in class.

ResultsPlus Controlled assessment tip

 Don't treat spontaneous spoken language as a lower form of written language. Think about the way you and the people around you speak. What forms do they use and what sounds appropriate?

ACTIVITY 2

1. Listen to a weather forecast on the TV or radio. This is an example of a scripted speech.

2. Have a conversation with your friends about the weather, or listen to the recorded conversation of two people talking about the weather available on the ActiveTeach. This is an example of spontaneous speech.

3. Make notes on any differences you noticed between the examples of spoken language.

In **spontaneous** spoken language, when someone speaks there will be **pauses**, or breaks in speech. The speakers may also say 'er' or 'um'. Speakers may pause because they are thinking what to say or because they are changing the subject. For example:

> I was lying in bed, **erm**, **I think … I think** it was probably about 11:00pm.

Sometimes speakers make **false starts**. This is when they start to say something and then change their minds and say something else. For example:

> **It was… it happened** yesterday.

Spoken language needs to communicate quickly. To do this, people shorten phrases – for example, they say 'dunno' instead of 'I don't know.' They can also leave sentences unfinished. This is called an **ellipsis**. For example:

> **Frank: Comin'**?
> **Brian**: Nah, not **gonna**.

Glossary for spoken language

spontaneous:
not planned

pauses:
breaks in speech

false start:
when speakers change what they are saying

ellipsis:
speaker shortens words or phrases

transcript:
record of spoken language

When we listen to a conversation it sounds normal, but if someone records that conversation and writes down everything that is said (a **transcript**), it can look rather odd.

There is no punctuation in transcripts, because people don't use punctuation when they speak. Marks like this (.) show places where the speaker has paused.

ACTIVITY 3

Below is a transcript of a man telling a story about a strange experience he had.

1 Look at the transcript, then copy and complete the chart below. Identify two pauses, a false start and an example of ellipsis (a shortened word or phrase).

2 Decide why each feature you identified has occurred. The first one has been done for you.

Feature	Example	Reason
Pause 1	to see him (.)	It's like punctuation because he's changing the subject a bit.
Pause 2		
False start		
Ellipsis		

When I was a young man I'd often heard the story of the grey monk (.) the ghost of the grey monk who travelled from the old monastery behind the church to t'church farm in Eastland's Lane (.) but I never expected that I should be able to see him (.) one night when I was cycling to work at about half past nine (.) this was in the days before electricity in Warsop and the street lamps were very few and far between only gas (.) and I was cycling to work as I would normally in a hurry turned off the A60 into the (.) Eastland's Lane and as my light went round the corner this six foot wall behind (.) beyond er six foot wall running be (.) beneath what was the rectory lawn in those days (.) the old rectory (.) and suddenly as I came round the corner my light shone on this figure (.) dressed in a grey long robe just gliding up the side of this six foot wall (.) my hair stood on end and just as suddenly as I'd seen him he disappeared (.) There was nothing there but oh (.) that's how it was (.) y'know it it it was there as plain as anything a long grey hooded figure robe right down to the foot (.) going along this wall there was no way out (.) nothing else there's a there's a bus shelter there now but there now but there wasn't then (.) it just went like that

People change how formally they speak according to the audience and situation. For example, you would use **formal** language to speak to your head teacher about an exam, but you would use **informal** language to speak to your friends about a party.

Often your language changes as the situation develops. You may be quite formal when you meet someone for the first time, but as you become more relaxed, your language becomes less formal.

Here are some features of formal and informal language in spoken language:

Informal language	Formal language
Slang	No slang
A lot of ellipsis	Fewer ellipses
First names and nicknames	Titles and surnames (e.g. Mr Brown)
Casual terms of address (mate, love)	More formal terms of address
Casual pronunciation ('h' dropping, missing final sounds off words, saying 'ca" instead of 'cat', or 'bo'le' instead of 'bottle')	More careful pronunciation
More non-standard English	More standard English

ACTIVITY 4

1 In each of the situations below, would you be likely to use formal or informal language? Why?

    a) Giving directions to a stranger

    b) Talking to a teacher

    c) Asking a sales person to find a top in your size

    d) Having your spoken language recorded

    e) Meeting someone for the first time

    f) A job interview

ResultsPlus Watch out!

■ Look closely at the spoken language and don't stereotype. Don't assume that adults always speak formally – they don't. Don't assume young people always use slang – they don't.

2 Understanding style and context

This lesson will help you to...

* understand how people change the way they speak (the style) depending on the situation

* identify and explain examples of the way context changes the way people speak

The way people speak is influenced by the situation they are in. This is called **context**.

Context includes the following:

Context	Explanation	Examples
Audience	**Who** you are speaking to	• How well you know them • What their status is • How old they are • Where they come from
Purpose	**Why** you are speaking	• Catching up with friends or family • Explaining something • Trying to persuade someone about something • Buying something in a shop
Situation	**Where** you are speaking	• Making a contribution in class • Making a debating speech • Being interviewed • Spending time with friends/family
Topic	**What** you are talking about	• Latest movie • Your science project • Why you should be given a job

ACTIVITY 1

Read the conversation below between a shopkeeper and a young man who is buying a pack of lager.

Young man: Just these, mate

Shopkeeper: Are you eighteen?

Young man: Um yeah hang on (gets out his driving licence)

Shopkeeper: (looks at driving licence) Cheers mate there you go

Young man: Cheers

1 How do they talk to each other?

2 How does the context affect the way they speak?

3 Is there any time when one speaker uses more formal language? Why?

There are other factors that affect the way people speak.

Factor	Explanation	Examples
Accent	How people pronounce words, based on where they are from	Someone from America will have a different accent from someone from England. Received Pronounciation, or Queen's English, is a social accent.
Dialect	Different vocabulary and grammar used in different regions	In Liverpool, people may say 'youse' instead of 'you'. In Yorkshire, people may say 'me boots' instead of 'my boots'.
Slang	Slang varies with age and background, and it changes all the time, especially among teenagers	Innit, blud, bling, diss, end of
Age	How you speak varies with age	Young children speak differently from older children and differently from adults.

ACTIVITY 2

1 Match the examples of spoken language below to the factor that is affecting the way it is said.

   a) She's wearin' cool gym shoes.

   b) We was wearin' cool trainers.

   c) He's got some bling trainers.

   d) He is wearing very sensible trainers.

Factors affecting the way people speak

- Age
- Slang
- Dialect
- Accent

ACTIVITY 3

1 Can you think of any times you have changed the way you speak to fit the context? Think about the different contexts you have been in: for example, at school with a teacher, at the cinema with friends, at dinner with your grandmother.

ResultsPlus Controlled assessment tip

⚠ Remember that everyone has a range of styles when they talk. No one is always formal and no one is always casual. Remember the *context*.

People generally speak in **conversations**. Having a conversation is one of the most skilful things we do because conversations move quickly and are quite complicated:

- speakers talk

- they then listen and understand

- they respond in the correct style and according to the context

- they take their turn to speak.

In a conversation, the following can occur:

Overlaps	When one person begins talking before the other has finished, or when two people try to take a turn at once
Interruptions	Sometimes another speaker will start their turn in the middle of someone else's turn
Repairs	It's possible to ask someone to repeat what they've said or make it clearer, even if it's not your turn to speak; people can also correct themselves if they've made a mistake
Feedback	When one person speaks, other people often make short responses and sounds, like 'mm', 'yeah', or 'right', to show they are listening

ACTIVITY 4

Look at the transcript below. It is from a conversation where one person is giving another directions. Words in bold between square brackets [ ] show that two people are speaking at once.

1 Identify an example of an overlap, a repair and feedback.

2 What do each of the features (overlap, repair and feedback) add to the conversation?

B: You get to some traffic lights (.) turn right at the traffic lights
[(.)] carry

A: huhuh

B: on down there that's the main road into York (.) just sort of carry on down there you'll come to some traffic lights keep in the right hand lane [(.)] and

A: Yeah

B: there are some traffic [**lights**]

A: [**What is**] it a dual carriageway then

B: Yes it's a dual carriageway (.) part of the way anyway

A: OK

B: If you carry er keep on the right hand lane [(.)] you

A: Yeah

B: come to some more traffic lights there's a roundabout there you'll see (.) erm (.) Clifford's Tower on the right

A: Wha- what's Clifford's Tower

B: Yes it's a big tower on a mound you'll be actually riding alongsi-on the road alongside Clifford's Tower (.) You're in York then.

Here is an example of a controlled assessment task you could be expected to answer.
In your response to this task you will be expected to use punctuation effectively.

> Using two examples of spoken language, comment on the way teenagers adapt their spoken language to suit the situation.
>
> You should comment on:
>
> • how the purpose of the spoken language affects the way it is used
>
> • how language use influences other speakers and listeners
>
> • the level of formality
>
> • the use of slang
>
> • who speaks most if there is more than one speaker.   (24 marks)

ACTIVITY 5

Write a response to the following question.

Using two different examples of teenagers' spoken language, when they are talking with their friends outside school and talking with their teachers in class, comment on some of the ways the purpose of the spoken language affects the way they speak.

You should spend 20 minutes on this task.

ResultsPlus Self assessment

Before you complete this self-assessment activity you might like to read some sample answers to this task on the following pages (168 – 169).

Check your answer to Activity 5:
• Did you give **examples** of spoken language features?
• Did you **explain** how these features relate to the purpose of the spoken language?
• Have you developed this explanation **clearly**?

Maximise your marks

Using two different examples of teenagers' spoken language, when they are talking with their friends outside school and talking with their teachers in class, comment on some of the ways the purpose of the spoken language affects the way they speak.

Here are three student answers to the writing about spoken language on page 165. Around and after the answers are examiner comments. Read both the student answers and examiner comments. Then complete the activity at the bottom of page 167.

Student 1 – Extract typical of a grade (E) answer

> A good observation, but this is too simple

Teenagers use informal language and adults use formal language. Teenagers don't speak properly and use slang like 'dunno' and swear sometimes and adults don't. We interrupt each other and we use pauses to think about what we are going to say.

> A good example of the observation, but incorrect

Examiner summary

This part of the answer is typical of a grade E performance. The student observes certain aspects of the language of teenagers, and gives an example, but makes the assumption that casual forms are all teenagers use. The observation that adult language is formal and teenage language is casual is simplistic and incorrect. This answer would be improved a great deal if the student showed more awareness of the different contexts in which teenagers speak and the way they adapt their language.

Student 2 – Extract typical of a grade (D) answer

> A good general point, but needs supporting with examples

When the three girls are talking to each other, they use a lot of casual language. They interrupt each other a lot and no one really talks more than anyone else. When they are talking to their teachers, they are more polite. The teacher says most and no one interrupts her.

> A good point, but it would be useful to know why

Examiner summary

This part of the answer is typical of grade D performance. The student shows a clear awareness that teenagers adapt their language when they are in different situations and gives some examples of how they might do this. Some more specific examples, to explain how the teenagers' language is more polite when they are talking to the teacher, would improve the answer.

ACTIVITY 3

Using what you have already learned about these characters from Texts A and B on pages 168 and 169, write a short scene showing EITHER:

1 Leanne and Rachel's conversation after they leave the cloakroom.

    a) What does Rachel say to Leanne?

    b) What does Leanne say? Does she explain why she was friendly to Sarah?

    c) How does Rachel react?

OR:

2 Albert and Alice's conversation.

    a) Is Albert embarrassed to find her sisters there?

    b) Is Alice upset that they haven't left her and Albert alone?

    c) Do either Vickey or Maggie try to join in the conversation?

Make sure you:

• **use the correct layout**

• **use stage or screen directions**

• **try to copy the way the characters you have chosen speak.**

ResultsPlus Controlled assessment tip

▲ Before you write your script, remember to think about your audience, purpose, medium and topic.

171

4 Writing dialogue

This lesson will help you to...

* write dialogue in narratives

* use dialogue to create characters and tell your story

You can use **dialogue** in a narrative to tell your story and reveal more about your characters.

When you write dialogue, put **speech marks** around the words characters would actually say:

> His footsteps slowed. 'I'm cold. Is it much further?'

You also need to say who is speaking:

> David looked up, surprised. 'What was that?' he said.

Change paragraph each time a new character speaks, and remember to punctuate your dialogue.

> 'So where are you going?' asked Matt.
>
> 'Just to the shop,' she answered.
>
> 'Would you mind getting me some soup?'

Below is an extract from *Of Mice and Men*, by John Steinbeck. Slim and George are talking about their friend, Lennie.

Slim sat down on a box and George took his place opposite.

'It wasn't nothing,' said Slim. 'I would of had to drowned most of 'em, anyways. No need to thank me about that.'

George said, 'It wasn't much to you, maybe, but it was a hell of a lot to him. Jesus Christ, I don't know how we're gonna get him to sleep in here. He'll want to sleep right out in the barn with 'em. We'll have trouble keepin' him from getting right in the box with them pups.'

'It wasn't nothing,' Slim repeated. 'Say, you sure was right about him. Maybe he ain't bright, but I never seen such a worker. He damn near killed his partner buckin' barley. There ain't nobody can keep up with him. God awmighty I never seen such a strong guy.'

ACTIVITY **1**

Look at the extract from *Of Mice and Men* on page 172.

1 Identify all examples of speech marks.

2 Identify all examples of words showing who the speaker is.

Dialogue helps to reveal details about characters. Through dialogue, you can:

- see the kind of language characters use – this shows where they are from, their age and how formal a situation they are in
- see how characters react to each other – this reveals their relationships.

Read the conversation below. Notice how the dialogue tells you more about the characters.

You can tell the girls are good friends by the way Sarah reacts to Gemma.

Slang shows the character is **young** and has an **English dialect.**

'Whoa,' Sarah gasped. 'That is the perfect dress, Gemma. You look hot!'

'Oh,' Gemma replied, doing an uncertain turn in the mirror. 'You really think? It's not too...too much?'

'Nah. It's wicked! I can see Lorna's face now. She's gonna be well jealous!'

Dialogue **builds the character,** showing that Gemma is self-conscious.

Shows the characters are talking **informally.**

ACTIVITY **2**

Read the extract from *Of Mice and Men* on page 172 again.

1 Find an example of dialogue that shows that George, Slim and Lennie are men, not boys.

2 Pick out an example of dialogue that shows the men are talking in an informal situation.

3 Find an example of dialogue that shows the story is set in America.

4 Find three examples of how dialogue reveals information about the characters' personality or their relationship. Write down each example, and explain what it reveals about the characters. The first one has been done for you.

> 'I don't know how we're gonna get him to sleep in here. He'll want to sleep out in the barn with 'em. We'll have trouble keepin' him from getting right in the box with them pups.'
>
> — You can tell George takes care of Lennie by the way he talks about him.

4 Writing dialogue

You need to make your dialogue seem real. To create successful dialogue, you need to:

- use appropriate language for the character and age of the person speaking. For example, a grandma wouldn't say 'butters'.

- make the dialogue seem natural. For example, say 'don't' and not 'do not'.

- keep your sentences informal in conversations among friends.

ACTIVITY 3

Read the dialogue below. It is unrealistic because people don't talk like this.

'What are you doing, Dave?' said Amir.

'I do not know,' Dave replied.

'I am sure you do,' said Amir. 'If you did not know, you would not be doing it.'

'I think you are right,' said Dave. 'I had better stop.'

'I think that is a good idea,' said Amir.

1 Rewrite the passage above, making the speech sound more realistic. Can you leave out any instances of 'said Dave' or 'said Amir' to make the writing better?

ACTIVITY 4

1 Write 100 to 150 words of a story with lots of direct speech. Ensure the dialogue:

- uses language that is appropriate for your characters – their age, how formal the situation is, where they are from

- has a purpose – it shows what's happening or tells more about character relationships

- is natural and realistic.

ResultsPlus Controlled assessment tip

 When writing dialogue, you don't need to say 'he said' or 'she replied' after every piece of dialogue, but make sure that your readers can follow who is speaking.

Here is an example of a controlled assessment task you could be expected to answer.

You will be expected to write in the form of a script and to use the conventions of scripting.

> **Write a script that contains between 30 seconds and 2 minutes of spoken language for a TV soap.**
>
> **(24 marks)**

ACTIVITY 5

Write a response to this question:

Write the opening section of your first scene. You should focus on the conventions of a TV script.

You should spend 20 minutes on this task.

ResultsPlus Self assessment

Before you complete this self-assessment activity you might like to read some sample answers to this task on the following pages (176 – 177).

Check your answer to Activity 5:
- Did you set your answer out using the proper **conventions for a script**?
- Did you include appropriate **direction**?
- Did you create realistic **dialogue**?
- Did you use the dialogue to create part of a story or narrative?

Maximise your marks

Write the opening section of your first scene. You should focus on the conventions of a TV script.

Here are three student answers to the TV script task on page 175. Around and after the answers are examiner comments. Read both the student answers and examiner comments. Then complete the activity at the bottom of page 177.

Student 1 – Extract typical of a grade Ⓔ answer

> Scene starts too quickly without background information

They start to fight.

A: S is doin my head in

S: Well J is accepting we live in a multicultural society

J: Look what he's done

All: Aaha

> Not very realistic dialogue

Examiner summary

This part of the answer is typical of grade E performance. The characters get involved in a fight immediately, before the audience have any understanding of what is going on. The characters don't have names, just initials, which increases the confusion. Some of the dialogue is not very realistic.

Student 2 – Extract typical of a grade Ⓓ answer

> Attempt at screen directions

> Attempt at screen directions

Vicky - what are you doing here

Sarah — walks over to Vicky

Sarah — I want a word with you you cow

Vicky swears at her

Vicky - Yeah what about

Sarah - You know

> Tries to create realistic dialogue

Examiner summary

This part of the answer is typical of grade D performance. The student has created some realistic dialogue and set it out as a script with some success. The characters' spoken words are indicated in two places, but in one place, the script is written more like a short story. There is no setting or context, so the story that is developing here is not easy to identify.

(In the interview room)

Opening sets the scene

Stevie: OK, Jack, the interview starts here.

Neil: This is your last chance, Jack. You can tell us your version.

Realistic dialogue

Jack: what do you mean? I told you the truth.

Neil: So you say.

Jack: Don't get clever with me (stands up)

Neil: Don't try anything, I'm warning you.

(Jack tries to hit him)

Scene moves a bit too fast

Examiner summary

This part of the answer is typical of grade C performance. The student has set this out as a script and has given some context so the developing story is easier to identify. The dialogue is in the appropriate form for a script, and there is a good attempt to make it realistic. However, the action moves a bit too fast. It might be better to have a little more development before the fight.

ResultsPlus
Build better answers

Move from a Grade Ⓔ to Grade Ⓓ
This answer needs to introduce the characters and the situation more effectively. You need to be aware of the story – what happens before your scene, what happens in the scene and what will happen afterwards.

Move from a Grade Ⓓ to Grade Ⓒ
In this part of your task you need to set your answer out like a script. You need to give appropriate directions and use realistic dialogue to develop your characters. You should keep your story in mind and make sure your script is following this.

PUTTING IT INTO PRACTICE

❶ Working in groups, perform your scripts. Is your script effective when it is read out?

❷ Make notes of what was effective in the scripts, and what didn't work so well.

Controlled Assessment Practice

Guidance for students: Spoken Language Study

What do I have to do?
You will complete one task on spoken language, from a choice of two. You must complete this task on your own.

How much time do I have?
Following preparation and research, you will have up to two hours to complete the task.

How do I prepare for the task?
You must research examples of spoken language. These may include:
* the language you hear around you
* a selection which could be taken from sources such as YouTube, TV or radio interviews, radio phone-ins or the British Library audio archives
* your or your school's own recorded materials.

You must provide two examples of spoken language to complete the chosen task. These examples can be taken from any of the sources. You will have to state the sources of the examples that you have used.

What must my response to the task show?
Your responses must show that you:
* understand how spoken language changes depending on the context, using examples
* understand some of the choices people make when they are speaking (for example: how they say it; what words or phrases they choose), using examples.

How should I present my response?
The response must allow you to show understanding of the examples of spoken language chosen. The response will be a written response of up to 1000 words to the task.

Examiner's tip

You need two examples. Try to think of two that are interesting to you and will give you material to discuss in your assessment.

Examiner's tip

You will need to comment on context and choice.

The Spoken Language Study Task for the student

You will complete one task from the two below:

EITHER

Using two examples of spoken language, comment on the way teenagers adapt their spoken language to suit the situation.

You should comment on:
- how the purpose of the spoken language affects the way it is used
- how language use influences other speakers and listeners
- the level of formality
- the use of slang
- who speaks most if there is more than one speaker.   (24)

OR

Using two examples of spoken language, comment on the differences between the speech of the area where you live and the speech of different places. (You may comment on one other place or more if you choose.)

You should comment on:
- how the purpose of the spoken language affects the way it is used
- how language use influences other speakers and listeners
- the level of formality
- the use of dialect
- the specific differences between the spoken languages being studied.
                                                          (24)

Examiner's tip

Pick one of these tasks. Try to focus on language that interests you.

Examiner's tip

Use these bullets to help you form and structure your response.

Guidance for students: Writing for the Spoken Voice

What do I have to do?
You will complete one task from a choice of three.

You must complete this task on your own.

How much time do I have?
Following preparation and research, you will have up to two hours to complete this task.

How do I prepare for the task?
You should watch, read and listen to examples of the way writers create spoken words. These may include:

- radio plays
- films
- TV drama
- radio and TV documentaries
- sitcoms

- radio advertisements
- graphic novels
- monologues
- speeches
- stand-up comedy.

What must the response to the task show?
The response must show that you:
- understand how a media type (radio, TV, graphic novels, etc.) works
- understand the needs of an audience and purpose.

How should I present the response?
As a written response that is effective for the form, purpose and audience chosen for the task.

Writing for the Spoken Voice Task for the student

You will complete one task from those below:

EITHER
Write a script that contains between 30 seconds and 2 minutes of spoken language for:
- a TV soap **OR**
- a graphic novel **OR**
- a radio drama.

Your script may be totally original **OR** may be for a TV soap, graphic novel or radio drama that already exists.

(24)

OR
Write a speech of up to 1000 words in support of a topic of your choice in a debate.

(24)

OR
Write a story of up to 1000 words in which direct speech is a key focus.

(24)

Examiner's tip

Select one task from these three. Use your creativity to make your writing for the spoken voice interesting.

Examiner's tip

Remember to make the language you use appropriate for the form you're writing in.

Published by Pearson Education Limited, a company incorporated in England and Wales, having its registered office at Edinburgh Gate, Harlow, Essex, CM20 2JE. Registered company number: 872828

Edexcel is a registered trade mark of Edexcel Limited

Text © Pearson Education Limited 2010

The rights of Clare Constant, Danuta Reah, Racheal Smith and Geoff Barton to be identified as authors of this work have been asserted by them in accordance with the Copyright, Designs and Patent Act 1988.

First published 2010

12 11 10
10 9 8 7 6 5 4 3 2

British Library Cataloguing in Publication Data
A catalogue record for this book is available from the British Library.

ISBN 978 1 84690 704 3

Designed and typeset by Juice Creative Limited, Hertfordshire
Printed and bound in Great Britain at Scotprint, Haddington

We would like to thank Tony Farrell for his invaluable help in the development of this material.

Picture Credits
The publisher would like to thank the following for their kind permission to reproduce their photographs:
(Key: b-bottom; c-centre; l-left; r-right; t-top)

Alamy Images: Paul Springett 03 90, Archives du 7eme Art / Photos 12, 172, Jeff Morgan 13 129, 149, Form Advertising 55, James Boardman 71, canadabrian 145, Kathy deWitt 9, Sindre Ellingsen 162, culture-images GmbH 59tl, ianmurray 109, 117, imagebroker 44, Evox Productions, LLC / Drive Images 16, Kelly Redinger / Design Pics Inc., 157, ACE STOCK LIMITED 143, MARKA 13, Trinity Mirror / Mirrorpix 169, Nigel Reed QEDimages 66, Image Source 168, Richard Wadey 72, Miglbauer / WoodyStock, 59r; **Barcroft Media**: 31b; **BBC Photo Library**: 98/2, 138; **Camera Press Ltd**: Robert Doisneau 154; **Getty Images**: Ben Stansall / Stringer 154/2, DESHAKALYAN CHOWDHURY / Stringer 31t; **iStockphoto**: 17, 39bl, 87, 89, 95, 126, Lance Bellers 170, John-Francis Bourke 171, Anna Bryukhanova 114, Rhienna Cutler 164, Diane Diederich 163, Giorgio Fochesato 160, Alberto L. Pomares G. 63, Francois Van Heerden 125, Andrea Hill 134c, Daniel Jensen 30, Brad Killer 90b, Robert Kohlhuber 112, Derek Latta 139t, David Lewis 41, Dejan Ljamic 175, Jim Lopes 134b, Milos Luzanin 74, Brian McEntire 98, Daniel Norman 43b, Maxim Petrichuk 134t, Chris Price 147, Chris Schmidt 103, Reuben Schulz 76, Stefan Schulze 39r, Hasan Shaheed 123, Nuno Silva 124, Catherine Yeulet 107; **Mother**: 11; **NHS Blood and Transplant**: 41/2; **Oxfam**: 17/2; **Pearson Education Ltd**: Pearson Education Ltd. Gareth Boden 92, 148, Pearson Education Ltd. Gareth Boden 92, 148, Imagestate. John Foxx Collection 80, 96, Imagestate. John Foxx Collection 80, 96, Fancy. Veer. Corbis 91, www.imagesource.com. Corbis 136t, Creatas 127, 128, Comstock Images 113, Pearson Education Ltd. Naki Kouyioumtzis 132c, Photodisc. Doug Menuez 66t, Pearson Education Ltd. MindStudio 67, 81, Photodisc 60, Pearson Education Ltd. Tudor Photography 125b, 158, 159, Pearson Education Ltd. Tudor Photography 125b, 158, 159, Pearson Education Ltd. Tudor Photography 125b, 158, 159, KPT Power Photos 59bl, Brand X Pictures. Burke Triolo Productions 78, Pearson Education Ltd. Debbie Rowe 132b, Pearson Education Ltd. Jules Selmes 161, Stockbyte 136b, National Geophysical Data Center. J.D. Griggs. Hawaii Volcano Observatory. U.S. Geological Survey 133, 135, Digital Vision 56, Photodisc. Karl Weatherly 104, www.imagesource.com. Nick White 79, Pearson Education Ltd. Studio 8. Clark Wiseman 136, 165, Pearson Education Ltd. Studio 8. Clark Wiseman 136, 165, www.imagesource.com 39tl; **Science Photo Library Ltd**: PASCAL GOETGHELUCK 10l, SOVEREIGN, ISM 10r; **The Prince's Trust**: 32/2, 33, 33/2, 33/3, 33/4, 33/5, 33/6, 33/7, 33/8, 33-34; **Veer**: Martin Crowdy 155; **War on Want**: Tarif Rahman 32; **Graham Watson**: 43

Cover images: Front: **iStockphoto**: Krzysztof Kwiatkowski

All other images © Pearson Education

Every effort has been made to trace the copyright holders and we apologise in advance for any unintentional omissions. We would be pleased to insert the appropriate acknowledgement in any subsequent edition of this publication.

Acknowledgements
We are grateful to the following for permission to reproduce copyright material:

Cartoons: Cartoon on page 41 from 'Facebook - you have 200001 friends' cartoon by Gary from article Why I hate Facebook by Janet Street Porter, http://www.dailymail.co.uk/news/article-1138445/Janet-Street-Porter-Why-I-hate-Facebook.html, Daily Mail.

Logos: Logo on page 15 from RoadSTARS logo, http://www.kingston.gov.uk/browse/transport_and_streets/road_safety/rbkroadstars.htm, Kingston Council and the RoadSTARS Student Council.

Screenshots: Screenshot on page 12 from Bullying puzzle poster, Rawmarsh City Learning Centre; Screenshot on page 12 from Why do people bully? poster, http://www.didax.com/support/images/2-166/2-166a.gif, Didax, Inc; Screenshot on page 14 from Freshwater Fishing Australia, Issue 89, March/April 2008, artwork of cover of Freshwater Fishing Australia magazine reproduced with permission from Australian Fishing Network; Screenshot on page 15 from Girl Talk magazine 24 feb – 9 march 2010 issue 394 (c) BBC Worldwide 2010 Girl Talk is a registered trade mark of the British Broadcasting Corporation; Screenshot on page 17 from The temperature displayed is 50c. Is the sausage cooked properly?, http://www.glasgows.co.uk/fsa_interactives/BBQload.swf, reproduced under the terms of the Click-Use Licence; Screenshot on page 17 from LG Cookie, http://www.mobile-phones-uk.org.uk/lg-kp500.htm, Landmark Internet Ltd; Screenshot on page 20 from Odeon 25% off voucher, with permission from ODEON/UCI Cinemas; Screenshot on page 21 from NSPCC home page, http://www.nspcc.org.uk/default.html, with permission from the NSPCC; Screenshot on page 22 from Fire Safety for Gypsies and Travellers, Communities and Local Government, June 2008 pp.

Websites

The websites used in this book were correct and up to date at the time of publication. It is essential for tutors to preview each website before using it in class so as to ensure that the URL is still accurate, relevant and appropriate. We suggest that tutors bookmark useful websites and consider enabling students to access them through the school/college intranet.

Disclaimer

This material has been published on behalf of Edexcel and offers high-quality support for the delivery of Edexcel qualifications.

This does not mean that the material is essential to achieve any Edexcel qualification, nor does it mean that it is the only suitable material available to support any Edexcel qualification. Edexcel material will not be used verbatim in setting any Edexcel examination or assessment. Any resource lists produced by Edexcel shall include this and other appropriate resources.

Copies of official specifications for all Edexcel qualifications may be found on the Edexcel website: www.edexcel.com